# Funny How?

THE SUNY SERIES

HORIZONS OF CINEMA

MURRAY POMERANCE | EDITOR

# Funny How?

## Sketch Comedy and the Art of Humor

Alex Clayton

Cover art: From left to right: Eric Idle, Graham Chapman, Michael Palin, John Cleese, Terry Jones, and Terry Gilliam. Columbia Pictures/Photofest.

Published by State University of New York Press, Albany

© 2020 State University of New York

All rights reserved

No part of this book may be used or reproduced in any manner whatsoever without written permission. No part of this book may be stored in a retrieval system or transmitted in any form or by any means including electronic, electrostatic, magnetic tape, mechanical, photocopying, recording, or otherwise without the prior permission in writing of the publisher.

For information, contact State University of New York Press, Albany, NY
www.sunypress.edu

### Library of Congress Cataloging-in-Publication Data

Names: Clayton, Alex, 1979– author.
Title: Funny how? : sketch comedy and the art of humor / Alex Clayton.
Description: Albany : State University of New York Press, 2020. | Series: SUNY series, horizons of cinema | Includes bibliographical references and index.
Identifiers: LCCN 2019028909 | ISBN 9781438478296 (hardcover : alk. paper) | ISBN 9781438478289 (pbk. : alk. paper) | ISBN 9781438478302 (ebook)
Subjects: LCSH: Comedy—History and criticism—Theory, etc. | Comedy sketches—History and criticism—Theory, etc.
Classification: LCC PN1922 .C525 2020 | DDC 809/.917—dc23
LC record available at https://lccn.loc.gov/2019028909

10 9 8 7 6 5 4 3 2 1

*For Sarah, Sylvie, and Fraser,*
*who make me laugh every single day*

# Contents

| | |
|---|---|
| List of Illustrations | ix |
| Preface | xiii |
| Acknowledgments | xv |
| Introduction | 1 |
| 1  The Trouble with Comic Theory | 9 |
| 2  Takeoffs | 49 |
| 3  Thought Experiments | 71 |
| 4  Prime Numbers | 89 |
| 5  Pitched Battles | 107 |
| Conclusion: The Rhetoric of Humor | 127 |
| Works Cited | 137 |
| Index | 139 |

# Illustrations

0.1  The Customer (John Cleese) is always right, except when he's wrong. Michael Palin is the Shopkeeper (left). *Monty Python's Flying Circus* (BBC, 1969–74, S1:E8).    2

0.2  "It's a stiff!" John Cleese, *Monty Python's Flying Circus* (BBC, 1969–1974, S1:E8).    5

1.1  Indiana Jones (Harrison Ford) brings a gun to a swordfight. *Raiders of the Lost Ark* (Steven Spielberg, 1981).    11

1.2  Nelson Muntz. *The Simpsons* (Fox, 1989–present).    16

1.3  Lou (David Walliams) seeks the ear of the pool attendant (Steve Furst). Andy (Matt Lucas) prepares to dash. *Little Britain* (BBC, 2003–06, S1:E1).    22

1.4  Lou fusses in the foreground and Andy leaps in the far ground. *Little Britain* (BBC, 2003–2006, S1:E1).    27

1.5  Simon Pegg is the petrified monk. *Big Train* (TalkBack Productions, 1998–2002, S1:E5).    28

1.6  From left to right: Mark Heap, Simon Pegg, Kevin Eldon. *Big Train* (TalkBack Productions, 1998–2002, S1:E5).    32

1.7  Keegan-Michael Key and Jordan Peele (extras uncredited). *Key and Peele* (Comedy Central, 2012–15, S5:E5).    34

1.8  Heads will turn. Keegan-Michael Key and Jordan Peele. *Key and Peele* (Comedy Central, 2012–15, S5:E5).    37

1.9 Shame. Jordan Peele. *Key and Peele* (Comedy Central, 2012–15, S5:E5). 39

1.10 The delusional Sir Digby (Robert Webb). *That Mitchell and Webb Look* (BBC, 2006, S1:E1). 41

2.1 Ted Striker (Robert Hays) struts his stuff in *Airplane!* (Jim Abrahams, David Zucker, and Jerry Zucker, 1980). 50

2.2 Ted (Robert Hays) must be dreaming. Barfly is uncredited. *Airplane!* (Jim Abrahams, David Zucker, and Jerry Zucker, 1980). 53

2.3 Ted (Robert Hays) busts some serious moves. *Airplane!* (Jim Abrahams, David Zucker, and Jerry Zucker, 1980). 55

2.4 Miss Babs (Celia Imrie) answers the phone at Acorn Antiques. *Victoria Wood: As Seen on TV* (BBC, 1985–87, S2:E3). 57

2.5 The marvelous Mrs. Overall (Julie Walters). *Victoria Wood: As Seen on TV* (BBC, 1985–87, S2:E3). 63

2.6 When is a wig too big? Mr. Pogg (Francis Greenslade), master of Spiffington Manse. *The Micallef Program* (ABC, 1998–2001, S2:E6). 65

2.7 Getting into a "tither." Anne Phelan, Francis Greenslade, Roz Hammond. *The Micallef Program* (ABC, 1998–2001, S2:E6). 67

3.1 Michael Palin and John Cleese. *Monty Python's Flying Circus* (BBC, 1969–74, S3:E3). 72

3.2 Curtain call: Michael Palin, Eric Idle, John Cleese, Graham Chapman, and Terry Jones. The hand about to emerge from the doorway may or may not belong to Terry Gilliam. *Monty Python's Flying Circus* (BBC, 1969–74, S3:E3). 76

3.3 I wanna be like you: Mel Smith and Rowan Atkinson. *Not the Nine O'Clock News* (BBC, 1979–82, S2:E5). 78

3.4 The guests take their seats. From left to right: François Maistre, Maryvonne Ricaud, Alix Mahieux, Marie-France Pisier, Jean Rougerie. *The Phantom of Liberty* (Luis Buñuel, 1974). 83

| | | |
|---|---|---|
| 3.5 | Nature calls. François Maistre. *The Phantom of Liberty* (Luis Buñuel, 1974). | 87 |
| 4.1 | Ernie Wise and Eric Morecambe. *The Morecambe and Wise Show* (BBC, 1968–77, S9:E6). | 90 |
| 4.2 | Eric Morecambe and Ernie Wise. *The Morecambe and Wise Show* (BBC, 1968–77, S9:E6). | 94 |
| 4.3 | Jerry Lewis. *The Errand Boy* (Jerry Lewis, 1961). | 96 |
| 4.4 | Jerry Lewis. *The Errand Boy* (Jerry Lewis, 1961). | 99 |
| 4.5 | Jerry Lewis. *The Errand Boy* (Jerry Lewis, 1961). | 100 |
| 4.6 | Jerry Lewis. *The Errand Boy* (Jerry Lewis, 1961). | 100 |
| 4.7 | Jerry Lewis. *The Errand Boy* (Jerry Lewis, 1961). | 101 |
| 4.8 | Eddie Murphy. *Saturday Night Live* (NBC, 1975–present, S9:E4). | 102 |
| 5.1 | Tim Brooke-Taylor, John Cleese, Graham Chapman, and Marty Feldman are the Four Yorkshiremen. *At Last the 1948 Show* (Associated Rediffusion, 1967, S2:E6). | 108 |
| 5.2 | Eric Wareheim is about to strike Tim Heidecker. *Tim and Eric Awesome Show, Great Job!* (Abso Lutely Productions, S4:E3, 2009). | 114 |
| 5.3 | Sally Phillips sings, and Doon Mackichan ignores. *Smack the Pony* (Fremantle Media, S1:E1, 1999). | 118 |

# Preface

This book is about sketch comedy, which might roughly be defined as a standalone comic episode or vignette of several minutes that has its own distinct line of development (beginning, middle, and end) and is typically acted out by a troupe of performers. My batch of case studies is drawn from film and television, and includes a few instances that some people perhaps wouldn't consider sketch comedy. I should say that I am not especially interested in policing the boundaries of the category, much more interested in comic achievement across a range of what could broadly be conceived as the sketch format. I make no claims for coverage: this is not a history of the sketch show, nor even a genre study. I have simply, unashamedly, chosen sketches that I love. Indulgent though I may be judged, this selection principle is absolutely necessary to what the book is about, which is the question of what makes something funny. Obviously, I'm in no position to say what makes something funny if I don't number amongst the group that finds it funny. And I figure I am on strongest ground to articulate the merits of sketches when I find them richly, brilliantly funny. There are examples here from Australia, France and the US, but most of the sketches discussed in the book are from the UK. Which is also where I'm from: I hope readers will forgive my parochialism.

One thing I discovered, in seeking my examples, is that a great comedy sketch is extraordinarily rare. Given the talent that has worked in this format, this tells me that sketch comedy is one of the toughest of comic challenges. At a bare minimum, you have to introduce your characters, set out your premise, offer some elaboration, variation, development, a new surprising direction, and close it out—all in typically less than four minutes. And, most importantly, it needs to be funny. How that has been achieved is the subject of this book. My commentary is offered to fellow enthusiasts of comedy, and perhaps also to aspiring comedians, although I should make clear this is no how-to-be-funny guide. I am too much in awe of the talent, intelligence and nerve of comic creators to offer practical advice for would-be comedians.

I wrote this book because I wanted to pay homage to those talents. This is, to my knowledge, the first single-authored book dedicated to the analysis of sketch comedy. There was another reason for writing it: I have been teaching comedy at the University of Bristol for more than a decade, and have been continually frustrated by the paucity of close textual criticism on comedy to assign as reading. Since I was setting the analysis of humor as an assignment for my students, I needed to offer some model, or at least an indication, of how one might go about that business. I hope students and devotees of comedy, of all ages, inside and outside the academy, find the book instructive and enjoyable.

I would highly recommend watching the sketches prior to reading my accounts of them. At the time of publication, the seventeen sketches discussed in depth are all available online and tagged with the search term *#funnyhow*.

# Acknowledgments

I would like to thank the University of Bristol for granting me research leave for this project at a key stage. Thanks also to the members of my Film and TV Comedy class of 2017, who were patient enough to listen and respond to an early version of this material (with special mention to Samuel Ireland who put me on to Tim and Eric's "Price War"). Murray Pomerance has been an exemplary editor. I am especially grateful for his annotations on draft material, his eye for detail, and his sense of humor. I would like also to thank Camille Hale, the elegant copyeditor of this volume, for fixing so many sentences and making me seem much more cleverer. Any errors, shortfalls, or missed opportunities are wholly my own.

# Introduction

> The crush of thoughts that do not get out, because they all push forward and get wedged in the door.
>
> —Ludwig Wittgenstein (1979: 3)

❦

IN WHAT IS PERHAPS THE MOST celebrated sketch of all time, a peeved customer (John Cleese) returns a faulty product to a local shop, seeking recompense for the item that he bought just half an hour before. The item in question is a parrot, and the fault in question is that it is dead. Stone dead. Expired. Passed on. It is an ex-parrot. All of which the shopkeeper (Michael Palin) casually refutes. The show is, of course, *Monty Python's Flying Circus* (BBC, 1969–1974, S1:E8). John Cleese has recounted the genesis of the Dead Parrot sketch:

> Michael [Palin] started to tell me about taking his car in to his local garage. He would ring the guy there and say, "I'm having trouble with the clutch." And this guy would say, "Lovely car, lovely car," and Mike said, "Well yes, it is a lovely car, but I'm having trouble with the clutch."
> "Lovely car, lovely car, can't beat it."
> "No, but we're having trouble with it."
> "Well, look," he says, "if you ever have any trouble with it, bring it in."
> And Michael would say, "Well, I *am* having trouble with it and I *have* brought it in."
> And he'd say, "Good, lovely car, lovely car, if you have trouble bring it in."

Figure 0.1. The Customer (John Cleese) is always right, except when he's wrong. Michael Palin is the Shopkeeper (left). *Monty Python's Flying Circus* (BBC, 1969–74, S1:E8).

And Michael would say, "No, no, no, the clutch is sticking."

And he would say, "Sign of a quality car, if you had a sticky clutch first two thousand miles, it's the sign of good quality." He was one of those people you could never get to take a complaint seriously.

Michael and I chatted about this, and I then went off and wrote a sketch with Graham [Chapman] about a man returning a second-hand car . . . That was early '68, so when we started to write over a year later for *Python*, I remember we looked at the sketch again. Both Graham and I agreed the car was much too hackneyed, and within a moment we were in a pet shop and we said, "Which is funnier, could it be a dog or a parrot?" We argued the toss—well, not argued, chewed that around a bit—and decided it was the parrot. (Chapman et al., 2003: 146)

If you put your mind to it, and it's quite a fun game, you can think of a dozen half-decent variants on this basic scenario. A rubber hammer being returned to a hardware store. A real hammer being returned to a joke shop. Two hats being returned to a shoe shop. A warhead returned by a minor-league dictator to his local munitions shop. So, why the pet shop, and why the parrot? Most obviously, perhaps, second-hand car salesmen have a (no doubt unfair) reputation for exploiting customers, whereas we might assume (perhaps also unfairly) the typical keeper of a pet shop to be an honest, congenial type. A pet shop is also more likely a neighborhood store than an impersonal chain or out-of-town locality where full-throated complaint would be easier to muster. Moreover, a pet shop is a peculiar type of shop since the "products" are (ideally) alive at the point of purchase and are expected to stay alive long enough to become companions. For reasons of sympathetic attachment, the exchange of an unwanted pet is not like the exchange of a faulty machine. These factors, along with no doubt several more, add richness and spice to the recipe of the brushed-off complaint.

Why, then, a parrot? Why not a dog—or, for that matter, a fish or a lizard? A dead dog, perhaps being dragged back into the pet shop on a lead, would doubtless create a grotesque quality. The mixture of disgust and sympathy, perhaps even distress, inspired by that image would threaten to overwhelm the premise. A dead fish, on the other hand, even an elaborate tropical fish, is not enough of a big deal, perhaps because pet fish are expected to be primarily decorative rather than companionate. Parrots, to split the difference, have lovely plumage, but they can also interact with you—which makes them companionate and decorative in roughly equal measure, or perhaps slightly more companionate than decorative. They can talk, after a fashion. In other words, they are not so companionate that the death of an unknown parrot could be felt tragic, but also not so simply decorative as to make it an impersonal matter of return-and-replace. There is also the matter of movement, which pertains to credibility. It's somewhat too credible, given the metabolism of the cold-blooded, that a dead lizard could be mistaken for a live lizard, even credible that the issue might, for a moment or two, be genuinely debatable. The same could not be said of a dead dog; we could scarcely believe Fido's new owner to have been so hoodwinked. A belly-up fish, on the other hand, for the uninitiated, might just about be mistaken for a live fish with the charming habit of swimming at the surface, upside-down. In terms of whether a customer could conceivably have gone through with the purchase and taken a full half hour to come back, it's got about the same degree of credibility as a nailed-to-the-perch parrot. That is, it's *barely* credible, but capable of being entertained—which is all that (and no more than) we need.

There is also the matter of the *sound* of the word "parrot." When John Cleese utters the phrase "Now that's what *I* call a dead parrot," having demonstrated his point by yelling at it, bashing it on the counter, and throwing it on the floor, he is able to slightly trill the "r," which draws out the character's haughtiness. "Dead dog" wouldn't allow this. There is also the rhythmic advantage of "parrot," with its equally stressed pair of syllables, over multisyllabic pets like "guinea pig" or "tarantula." The phrase "Now that's what *I* call a dead parrot," as delivered by Cleese, has an end-of-chorus feel. It caps his brutal demonstration with the cadence of a music-hall ditty.

As the above remarks hopefully start to suggest, playing the hypothetical alternative game is one of the best ways to start analyzing instances of humor. It is also one of the more productive methods of aesthetic analysis in general. If you want to understand why something is funny—or, more generally in art, why something is *right*—the surest way to edge towards it, once you've found an instance that *feels* right, is to imagine how the thing might have been done slightly differently. The issue of moving parts invariably arises, since, in reality, if an artist changes one thing in the design, consequences follow, such that other things would probably have to be changed too. However, trying to trace the chain of these consequences can also be instructive. In fact, precisely because it mirrors the creative process, there is no more direct route into the artistic (in this case, comedic) imagination. Think of Cleese's reference to "chewing it around." As the next chapter will argue, however, this approach runs counter to that typically suggested by comic theory, which historically has tended to see humor in terms of a single psychological trigger point, or dualistic binary clash, rather than as the combination of countless things in concert.

Against the view that humor has an essence, it is the argument of this book that humor is irreducibly compound, and our historical failure to see it as such means that, for all these years, we have barely started to understand what makes something funny. E. B. White and Katharine S. White, in an oft-recited statement, declared that "humor can be dissected, as a frog can, but the thing dies in the process and the innards are discouraging to any but the purely scientific mind" (1941: xvii). This aphorism is often taken to cast doubt on the very possibility of analyzing humor. What it suggests to me, however, is that we need to abandon the idea of dissection altogether and engage in more careful field observation, to study how comedy behaves "in the wild." If analysis kills humor, then, to my mind, it suggests a faulty approach that fails to pay due heed to its object. Rather than considering the way multiple elements are variously selected and combined, the standard practice has been to theorize the essence of humor and then to ransack actual instances of humor for confirmation of the theory. This is a case of flogging a dead parrot.

Indeed, it is the very *density* of comedy that rewards being "chewed around." Here is another example from the same *Monty Python* sketch, a line delivered by John Cleese's now thoroughly exasperated customer in response to the shopkeeper's insistence that the parrot is either "resting" or "stunned":

> CUSTOMER: Look my lad, I've 'ad just about enough of this. That parrot is definitely deceased, and when I bought it not 'alf an hour ago, you assured me that its lack of movement was due to it bein' tired and shagged out after a long squawk.

There are important elements of performance that contribute to the humor here, including the curious accent Cleese adopts for his character, who sounds like a Cockney inexplicably putting on a posh voice, reminiscent perhaps of the la-di-da tea lady (Joyce Carey) in *Brief Encounter* (1945). The oddness of it is especially strong at this point, since the line combines starchy language (e.g., "you assured me," "due to it") with telltale colloquialisms and the habitual dropped "h." There is also the man's strange costume, an unencumbered medium closeup view of which is for the first time available as he delivers the line. It consists of a grey translucent Macintosh coat buttoned up to the neck, complementing his obsessively combed, side-parted hair to complete the appearance of a

Figure 0.2. "It's a stiff!" John Cleese, *Monty Python's Flying Circus* (BBC, 1969–1974, S1:E8).

fastidiously neat fellow on the verge of mania. There is also an important rhythmic component to the way the line has been crafted, with self-conscious literariness, and in the way it is delivered, culminating after all with the blunt and onomatopoeic word "squawk." But I want to call special attention to the density of suggestion in a couple of phraseology choices in the line I've just quoted.

What does it mean to say that a parrot is "deceased," for instance? One of the sketch's side ventures is to give Cleese more than a dozen elaborate ways of saying that the parrot is dead:

> CUSTOMER: It's bleedin' demised . . . It's passed on. This parrot is no more. It has ceased to be. It's expired and gone to meet its maker. This is a late parrot. It's a stiff! Bereft of life, it rests in peace. If you hadn't nailed it to the perch, it would have been pushin' up the daisies. It's run down the curtain and joined the choir invisible. THIS IS AN EX-PARROT!

Why is this done? There's an idea here about the redundancy of literary expression, a needless array of separate phrases for the same blasted thing—death! Each of these euphemisms, standing together in a kind of circle, faces inward toward the empty center to which they all, somewhat hopelessly, point. But there's also a contradictory suggestion that every word means something different—we might even say that there is no such thing as a synonym. It's not the same thing at all; hence it is funny to put them in the same sentence, to say that a parrot has "expired" and that it has "gone to meet its maker." The former typically refers to the perishing of food and other consumables, where the latter invokes ideas of divinity and the afterlife. The idea that a parrot is like a tin of beans is as absurd, in a different direction, as saying that a parrot will be received at the pearly gates. The word "deceased," to return to our earlier quoted line, contains a faint idea of the worthiness of an individual life, a sense that is manifestly not available in "bleedin' demised" or "pushin' up the daisies." The token respectfulness in "deceased," with its odor of the funeral parlor, is then immediately set at odds with reference to the transaction ("when I bought it not 'alf an hour ago") that casts the dearly departed as nothing more than a commodified beast. The incompatibility of commemoration and commerce is brought into play here. Then there is the phrase "shagged out," another beleaguered synonym, the redundancy of which is even more marked since it is structured as an addition ("tired *and* shagged out"). Notionally, "shagged out" is simply another way of saying "tired," its literal sense of sexual exhaustion having, at some historical point, moved to the background.

Perhaps the customer is directly quoting the shopkeeper's earlier excuse for the bird's lack of movement, an explanation improvised on the spot where the extraneous use of colloquialism might rhetorically have served to indicate that avian languor is quite normal (a joke in itself, since birds tend not to be languorous at all). With this attribution ("shagged out"), we are once again in the realm of anthropomorphism. The English tend to speak of human beings, not animals, as "shagged out," normally in the first person, most usually with reference to a hard day's graft rather than in the literal sense of sexual fatigue. The ideas commingle. The phrase "shagged out after a long squawk" combines the notion that a long squawk would be the parrot equivalent of a long day in the office with the equally pungent suggestion of the squawk as a mating cry, even as an orgasmic outburst, an ejaculation so violent it has laid the old bird cold—postcoitus as *rigor mortis*, a "stiff."

All of this is meant to do no more than to inaugurate the project of this book and what it wants to inspire in its readers: the inclination to pay due heed to the laughable, the faith that multitudes are contained within a comic nutshell. It should hopefully by now be obvious why sketch comedy is the ideal test case for this project. The compacting of ideas that I take to be a feature of all humor is most especially pronounced, even more compacted than usual, in this short- or micro-form genre. The term "sketch" could, for some, I suppose, suggest something dashed off in distinction to (or in preparation for) more substantial work. But, to my mind, the term "sketch" stands more positively for an intense economy of ideas borne from something ostensibly casual: the capacity to conjure a whole philosophy, no less, from a few choice lines and gestures.

# 1

# The Trouble with Comic Theory

WHY DO WE LAUGH? IS THE question at the heart of comic theory, by which I mean attempts to characterize the nature of laughter and humor, such as have appeared in essays and philosophical tracts stretching back to ancient times. John Morreall's collection *The Philosophy of Laughter and Humor* (1986) is the essential primer for this constituted field. Comic theory is very often taken, in academic and popular discussions of comedy, to represent a way of helping us to understand what makes something funny. It would certainly seem reasonable to expect a body of theory dealing with the question of why we laugh to be of some assistance in this task. Students of comedy are accordingly invited to set about analyzing instances of humor using comic theory as an imaginary toolbox. This chapter will show, however, that this approach is not likely to help us satisfactorily explain why something is funny, and is more likely to be actively unhelpful.

To understand why, we need first to consider the main schools of thought in comic theory. Following Morreall (1986) and others, comic theory is usually divided into three types, namely superiority theory, incongruity theory, and relief theory. The school of thought known as the superiority theory is perhaps epitomized by a well-known passage from Thomas Hobbes which claims that "the passion of laughter is nothing else but sudden glory arising from some sudden conception of some eminency in ourselves, by comparison with the infirmity of others, or with our own formerly" (2010 [1650]: 65). The figure of the fool and the phenomenon of ethnic humor are two areas where this notion has been thought to be pertinent. We laugh at a fool, so the presumption goes, because we find ourselves smarter or more agile than him. The classic Fool character knowingly carries out a task ineptly or presents himself as ignorant or unsophisticated, with an eye to flattering his audience. Similarly, we laugh at the stereotype of a foreigner because in our ethnocentrism we find the practices and tendencies represented by that depiction inferior to our own. In each case, humor is thought to offer a kind of massage to the ego, bolstering a pre-existing sense of cultural or personal superiority.

Hobbes finds people who laugh at such humor voracious in their appetite for a confirmation of self-worth: "greedy of applause from every thing they do well" (2010 [1650]: 65). This is to propose that engaging with a work or performance of humor involves a continuous process of self-other comparison. However, in his formulation, Hobbes adds the superiority he says we indulge may be "by comparison . . . *with our own formerly*" (2010 [1650]: 65, italics added). This allows the theory to accommodate less tendentious forms of humor, such as wit. Clever wordplay, for instance, might precipitate laughter because we recognize in triumph a connection we had formerly neglected. We thus become superior *now* to a *previously* inferior self. And this has to happen in an instant, for the glory to be "sudden."

An example might be the famous comic moment in *Raiders of the Lost Ark* (Steven Spielberg, 1981) when archaeological adventurer Indiana Jones (Harrison Ford) finds himself besieged in a bustling Cairo marketplace. The market throng parts to reveal a fearsome-looking Arab swordsman (Terry Richards), dressed in black with a red sash and brandishing an enormous scimitar, which he throws from hand to hand and starts to swing intimidatingly around his body. The crowd seems to be gearing up for a bout of hand-to-hand combat. To our surprise, however, Indy just takes a pistol from his holster and shoots the swordsman dead.

One might speculate, following the logic of the superiority theory, that our hypothetical viewer's laughter is prompted by a kind of sadistic glee at the swordsman's failure to observe that his foe has a gun. Perhaps our viewer has further been flattered by association with the hero's virtues—for instance, composure and a "cut-the-crap" ethos. For Indy's action of firing his pistol is not just a way of dispensing with an enemy but also a comment on the swordsman's vanity and profligacy. Moreover, one might speculate that the image of the quick-draw American vanquishing a Middle Eastern goon is capable of mobilizing, for members

Figure 1.1. Indiana Jones (Harrison Ford) brings a gun to a swordfight. *Raiders of the Lost Ark* (Steven Spielberg, 1981).

of a US audience, especially, certain notions of cultural superiority. The Arab stereotype here is of a pointedly medieval variety. In which case, the viewer's identification might be not just with the hero as personal surrogate, but with the triumph of US imperialism, framed as the ascendancy of the New World over the Old.

Hobbes's theory might further lead us to speculate that our viewer is able to feel superior *by comparison to his former self*, with regard to Indy's "solution" to the threat posed by the swordsman. *Of course* Indy was packing heat! The viewer had even been given a close-up of the pistol in an earlier sequence when Indy fatefully packed it in his luggage. In fact, the immediate lead-in to the sequence artfully conceals, makes us forget, that Indy has a gun. Obscured by movement, shadow, posture, and the careful selection of camera angle, blending into the grays of his pants and camouflaged by his shoulder bag, the pistol strapped to Indy's waist is visible in none of the lead-in shots, and Indy is cropped at the waist in the crucial reaction shot, so the brass button of the leather holster becomes visible at the bottom of the frame *only* when he pops it open. Nonetheless, our hypothetical viewer may feel that she has neglected the obvious, prompting the Hobbesian contrast: "What a fool was I! No more."

An alternative explanation of laughter at the Indy moment might be suggested by the relief theory of laughter. This school of thought is typified by John Dewey's remark that laughter "marks the ending . . . of a period of suspense, or expectation" and is simply "a sudden relaxation of strain, so far as occurring through the medium of the breathing and vocal apparatus . . . a phenomenon of the same general kind as the sigh of relief" (2008 [1889]: 158). In adherence to the laws of physics, any buildup of energy, the theory goes, must find some means of discharge. The idea is that the effort we have exerted in being concerned about an outcome, or the type of attention we have hitherto paid to the set-up of a joke or situation, is suddenly, on a punchline, rendered superfluous. Laughter is what issues forth when the release valve is activated. This hydraulic picture of the human was developed a few decades earlier by Herbert Spencer, for whom laughter was the product of "an undirected discharge of nervous energy into the muscular system" (in Morreall 1986: 105), and which would in turn come to inform the theories of Sigmund Freud, for whom laughter was the licensed venting of repressed feeling (Freud 1922). This would suggest an explanation of taboo humor, for instance, as providing momentary relief from the pressures of social prohibition on what cannot be thought, said, or enjoyed in polite company.

Returning to our example from *Raiders of the Lost Ark*, perhaps some latent sadism, even suppressed ethnic hostility, is momentarily licensed through Indy's shooting of the Arab. The culturally repressed viewer seeks some outlet for illicit and pent-up feelings, which the moment duly provides. On a more fundamental level, we might observe how the lead-in to the moment has worked to generate suspense, only for that tension to be all at once lifted. As the swordsman swings his weapon, brass alerts and dramatic flourishes on the soundtrack signal that he represents a new and severe threat (contrasting with the lighter, jauntier music that had thus far accompanied Indy's progress through the market). Moreover, the swordsman's virtuosity is being stressed in contrast to Indy's visible weariness. If all this suggests the cards are stacked against Indy, the surprise gunshot is like the production of the winning ace. The dramatic problem is suddenly solved, and our viewer's relief takes the form of laughter.

A further alternative line of approach might be suggested by the incongruity theory. This school of thought might be exemplified by Arthur Koestler's notion of "bisociation," which posits that amusement results from the perception of something in two incompatible frames of reference at the same time (Koestler 1964). Elsewhere, as Morreall summarizes it, incongruity theory suggests that amusement is "an intellectual reaction to something that is unexpected, illogical or inappropriate in some other way" (1983: 15). Something confounds our predictions, for instance, or someone fails to act according to custom. In the *Raiders of the Lost Ark* moment, the viewer, guided by local signals in the sequence, generates a hypothesis that a sustained fight scene will unfold—only for that assumption to be overturned. What transpires is incongruous with our expectation. It is incongruous in a different way, too—illogical, perhaps—that the swordsman wields his weapon with such confidence without first checking whether his rival has a gun. Moreover, Indy's shooting of the swordsman may be perceived as acting contrary to societal norms, here the code of the duel, as established by the way the crowd forms an oval around the combatants, anticipating hand-to-hand combat. In that sense, it could be perceived as "inappropriate." At the same time, however, it could be seen as "appropriate," in that it is highly effective, and the relation between "appropriate" and "inappropriate" creates its own incongruity. Perhaps, moreover, the action can be simultaneously seen in two generic frames of reference: that of the Eastern swordplay film (or associated genres), where a duel is a test of physical strength and dexterity, and that of the Western, where a duel takes the form of gun-slinging. And here there may nestle a further incongruity, since Indy's action might be construed as simultaneously moral and immoral: moral, in the sense that this goon is helping the Nazis, so Indy's violence is "justified," but it is also immoral within the terms of the Western, where shooting an (effectively) unarmed man is typically the act of a coward.

Each of these theories asks us to entertain different reasons why a viewer of this moment might laugh. However, to the extent that we find ourselves suggesting what a single, particular, hypothetical viewer *might* have thought and felt, the discussion can only remain cagey and speculative. To speak with authority about *other* people's responses, without consulting them, is to risk presumptuousness. Of course, one could ask them—but then what frame of reference would they use to construct their articulation? It's *difficult* to say what makes something funny. We would be back to square one.

As the above discussion has shown, engaging these theories does allow one to observe certain things about comic instances. However, the analysis is severely limited by the ostensible function of textual description to supply grounds for a hypothetical response, whether a sense of superiority, feelings of relief, or a perception of incongruity. Concrete observations can only be couched in speculation about what a viewer *may* think or feel. The problem arises because there is a mismatch between the kinds of hypotheses these theories offer and the kind of explanation we would require for a satisfying account of humor. The standard categorization of these theories into "schools of thought," as if you need to choose your team, obscures this problem. I would propose to slice the field another way, according to *different kinds of explanation*. There are at least five senses of the question Why do we laugh?:

1. Causal: How is laughter brought about? A technical question that asks what stimulus triggered the laughter.

2. Motivational: To what end do we laugh? A teleological question that asks with what intent laughter is imbued.

3. Functional: What are the advantages of laughter? An empirical question about the role of laughter, say in therapeutic terms, in terms of social organization, or in the evolution of our species.

4. Perceptual: Why do we find things funny? A psychological question that asks why individuals apprehend something *as* comic.

5. Aesthetic: How is $x$ funny? A clarificatory question that asks for an evaluative re-description of the comic object to which laughter is directed, of its various attributes, and how they are harmonized to work with one another in this "funny" particular way.

Each sense of the question suggests a different direction and conjures a different picture of laughter. The causal question pictures laughter as a reflex or compulsion. The motivational question pictures laughter as a kind of speech act, implying that by laughing we make to alter a state of affairs. The functional question pictures laughter as fulfilling a wider role, perhaps unseen, in the smooth running of our lives. The perceptual question pictures laughter as the expression of a humorous way of seeing. The aesthetic question, meanwhile, pictures laughter as an appreciation. Now, it is quite possible for us to be interested in more than one of these senses. But it is also important to recognize when the senses are being conflated or when an answer is being offered that misses the relevant sense of the question it purports to address.

We can find a clear instance of the question being taken in a causal sense in Dewey's physiological description, for example, where laughter is produced by "a sudden relaxation of strain, so far as occurring through the medium of the breathing and vocal apparatus" (2008 [1889]: 158). Note that to achieve a causal account, Dewey must minimize the volition of the laughing subject, which he does by denying her an attributive verb. It is laughter itself that "marks the ending . . . of a period of suspense," and relaxation of strain is reported as simply "occurring." It is common to find reference to "the cause of laughter" in comic theory, but that word "cause" has rarely been put under proper scrutiny. We speak of something "making us laugh," as if laughter were an unfortunate and involuntary spasm. But this picture of inducement is for the most part a trap of language. As soon as any such claimed response is elaborated, some degree of volition tends to edge back into the frame. We aren't quite puppets strung along by the jokester puppeteer: we have the agency to act. Even the laughter provoked by tickling, that prototype of causal accounts, requires an element of voluntary submission to the tickler. Besides, there is a mistake in conflating "automatic" and "spontaneous" laughter. Suppose an inventor came up with a machine that used electrical probes to stimulate the nervous system and incite laughter in a patient. This automatic laughter would bear as much resemblance to spontaneous laughter as the automatic tears produced by peeling onions bear to spontaneous tears of grief.

More often in comic theory, and in accounts and applications of comic theory, different senses of the question Why do we laugh? are conflated. For example, Arthur Schopenhauer, an influential proponent of the incongruity theory, postulates that "the cause of laughter in every case is simply the sudden perception of the incongruity between a concept and the real objects which have been thought through it in some relation, and laughter itself is just the expression of this incongruity" (2000 [1883]: 76). Here, the stimulant-reflex process implied by the term "cause" sits oddly with the picture of someone who, having "thought through" a certain relation between objects and concepts, gives "expression" to that perception in the form of laughter. This is really an account of why someone might *find* something funny, in other words, a perceptual account dressed up as a causal account.

Hobbes's explanation for laughter might also appear at first glance to be a causal account, when he writes that "the passion of laughter is nothing else but sudden glory *arising from* some sudden conception of some eminency in ourselves, by comparison with the infirmity of others, or with our own formerly" (2010 [1650]: 65, italics added). The phrase "arising from" invokes a causal process in vaguely mystical terms: first comes the "conception of eminency," from which arises the "passion of laughter." However, Hobbes is, like Schopenhauer, really offering a perceptual account. He is hypothesizing that laughter expresses a particular kind of perception (or "conception"). Those who laugh, who perceive in this way, are "greedy of applause from every thing they do well" (2010 [1650]: 65). This suggests, after all, that laughter is not a reflex ("arising from") but the willed expression of a way of seeing.

Functional accounts of laughter, meanwhile, are found frequently in anthropological and evolutionary explanations and in accounts that highlight the social or therapeutic benefits of humor. Laughter may be found to lubricate social relations, support group identity, or provide temporary relief from hardship. We might recall the chain gang at the end of *Sullivan's Travels* (Preston Sturges, 1941), seated on church pews, laughing their socks off together at a Mickey Mouse cartoon: comedy as the opium of the masses. Laughter might even, some have suggested, manifest a distant echo of primitive instincts that served a function in the evolution of our species. Matthew Gervais and David Sloan Wilson, for instance, have proposed that early hominids may have used laughter as kind of "vocal grooming," to secure social bonds between group affiliates (2005: 420).

All five senses of the question Why do we laugh? are engaged, without their differences being acknowledged, in what is perhaps the primary touchstone of comic theory, Henri Bergson's "Laughter: An Essay on the Meaning of the Comic" (2005 [1901]). Bergson's main thesis is that laughter serves a social purpose by holding over each member of a society "if not the threat of correction, at all events the prospect of a snubbing" (66). "By the fear which it inspires," he writes, "it restrains eccentricity . . . and, in short, softens down whatever the surface of the social body may retain of mechanical inelasticity." Laughter works to highlight "a certain rigidity of body, mind and character, that society would still like to get rid of in order to obtain from its members the greatest possible degree of elasticity and sociability. This rigidity is the comic, and laughter is its corrective." (17) This is a consistent social-functionalist account. It is when Bergson extrapolates from function to motive that his claims become dubious. The slippage occurs on the inference that,

Figure 1.2. Nelson Muntz. *The Simpsons* (Fox, 1989–present).

if laughter "pursues a utilitarian aim of general improvement" (17), then each individual act of laughter must be "intended to humiliate" (92).

The notion of laughter as enacting a humiliation might bring to mind schoolyard bully Nelson Muntz from *The Simpsons* (Fox, 1989–present) with his characteristically high-pitched "HA-ha," delivered as a descending major third and with an outstretched finger targeted at, for instance, in quick succession, a girl's new haircut, a woman falling into a bin, and a very tall man driving an economy car (S7: E21, "22 Short Films about Springfield"). It is surely true to say that Nelson's laughter is intended to humiliate, although with the Bergsonian twist that his own laughter is robotic and unvarying. But does it make sense to take Nelson's laughter as the archetype of all forms of laughter? For one thing, this would seem to disregard other possible motivations for (social) laughter, such as politeness (e.g., at the boss's jokes) or the demonstration of knowledge (e.g., laughing to signal that you recognize an esoteric reference). Moreover, it immediately rubs up against those occasions on which the object of our laughter is out of earshot. When I witness, in Jacques Tati's *Trafic* (1971), what appears to be documentary footage of a succession of drivers absent-mindedly picking their noses, there is no ontological possibility of my humiliating them by laughing. Perhaps with my vocal utterance I intend to send a warning to my fellow audience members (assuming I am not watching the film alone) that nose-picking or absent-mindedness in any form will be (in reality) subject to humiliation in the form of laughter. However, if sending this signal were my express intention, I would surely know of it, and we should hardly need a theory. It is for this reason that Bergson turns to the rescuing idea that our laughter "always implies a *secret* or *unconscious* intent . . . In laughter we always find an *unavowed* intention to humiliate, and consequently to correct our neighbor" (66, italics added). Setting aside the suspicion that "unconscious intent" is oxymoronic, the notion that we are all in denial of our true motivations for laughter is difficult to swallow (although impossible to disprove).

At any rate, this attribution of a motive for ostensibly spontaneous laughter is at odds with various causal claims made by Bergson in the course of his essay. Take, for instance, his italicized claim that *"we laugh every time a person gives us the impression of being a thing"* (33). "Every time" suggests an automatic response. Input: output. Yet elsewhere in the essay Bergson wants to stress that laughter is entirely contingent on the company we happen to be keeping (11). If laughter simply issued on receipt of a particular impression, then it is difficult to see how it could also be propelled by the motive to "correct our neighbor." One might put this down to rhetorical overstatement on Bergson's part. But the conflation goes deeper. Bergson insists even more stridently on the automatic nature of our laughter later when he claims it to be "simply the result of a mechanism set up in us by nature or, what is almost the same thing, by our long acquaintance with social life" (93). A generous reading might infer from the reference to "our long acquaintance with social life" that what Bergson has called "unconscious intent" could be redescribed as social habit. Yet Bergson again insists on laughter as an unwilled reflex: "It goes off spontaneously," he adds (93). That seems to leave little room for motive. Moreover, it makes laughter sound suspiciously like the kind of automatism that laughter is supposed to correct, presumably setting off further laughter. Witness the image of a society in perpetual convulsion.

This mechanical picture of laughter is at odds again with Bergson's discussion of "the logic of the laughable." At one particularly inspired point in that discussion, he claims that "the reasonings at which we laugh are those we know to be false, but which we might accept as true were we to hear them in a dream." (88) Here, Bergson has moved to a perceptual account of humor, an account of our cognitive and emotional grappling with works of comedy. There is now no talk of causal triggers ("simply the result of a mechanism") or of underlying motives ("an unavowed intention to humiliate"). Instead, what is offered is an explanation of why we might *find* certain things funny, of the mental disposition by means of which a particular text or performance comes to be seen as laughable. Finally, Bergson sometimes slips into treating the question "why do we laugh" as an aesthetic one. For example, when he claims that "any arrangement of acts and events is comic which gives us, in a single combination, the illusion of life and the distinct impression of a mechanical arrangement" (38), Bergson is primarily making an aesthetic claim, albeit a generalized one, about the "arrangement" of comic works, about what makes them funny, rather than a claim about the disposition or motive of hypothetical readers and viewers who laugh. If these many different impulses and potential contradictions are obscured in Bergson's essay, it is due to the deftness with which he navigates their conflicting directions. This seems to have dazzled investigations of humor in its wake, which have tended to presume, for instance, that a theory proposing an answer to the question What is the function of laughter? should naturally help answer the question What makes *this* funny? The latter is an aesthetic question, which calls in turn for an aesthetic explanation.

What, then, is an aesthetic explanation? Ludwig Wittgenstein describes this as "the sort of explanation one longs for" when puzzled about an aesthetic impression (1966: 19). This puzzlement takes the form of being at a loss to say how a work of art (or more broadly any sensate object or experience) has led you to a particular feeling, sensation, or judgment. However, this is not a question of determining a cause. Wittgenstein notes that if you want to know the basis of an aesthetic judgment, "the word 'cause' is hardly ever used at all. You use 'why?' and 'because,' but not cause." (14) Wittgenstein gives the (admittedly quirky) example of someone reporting his unease when walking through a doorway where the frame has been set too low: "There is a 'Why?' to aesthetic discomfort, not a cause . . . We have here a kind of discomfort which you may call 'directed' " (14). Similarly, it is helpful in aesthetic circumstances to think about laughter as *having direction* rather than as having been provoked by a stimulus or as the expression of something inner. It is an appreciation, perhaps a kind of spontaneous aesthetic judgment. Wanting to know "why we laugh" in this sense means wanting to know the basis for that judgment, trying to get a clearer view of what we are laughing *at*.

As an example of an aesthetic question, Wittgenstein gives the case of wondering about an enigmatic passage of music: "Why do these bars give me such a peculiar impression?" (20). Today, we might readily defer to neuroscientific descriptions of how brain networks respond to certain types of stimuli under certain conditions. Yet this would not answer an aesthetic question *in the relevant sense*. Importantly, this is not (as is sometimes claimed) because scientific research in this area has not yet reached a state of advanced knowledge or that measurements are not yet sufficiently fine-tuned. Wittgenstein offers a thought experiment to make this point:

> Suppose . . . we discovered particular kinds of mechanism in the brain [to] show that the sequence of notes produces this particular kind of reaction; makes a man smile and say, "Oh, how wonderful." Suppose this were done, it might enable us to predict what a particular person would like and dislike. We could calculate these things. The question is whether this is the sort of explanation we should like to have when we are puzzled about aesthetic impressions, e.g. there is a puzzle—"Why do these bars give me such a peculiar impression?" Obviously it isn't this, i.e. a calculation, an account of reactions, etc., we want—apart from the obvious impossibility of the thing. (20)

It would, of course, be an amazing accomplishment if a level of scientific knowledge were reached whereby we could accurately predict whether or not a given person will laugh at a particular joke. Perhaps the machine for calculating this likelihood could be called the Laugh Predictor 3000™.

Comedians would obviously find this technology invaluable. Perhaps it could also have a reverse gear that could specify what environmental and biological factors were salient when I laughed at a particular joke. This would offer one kind of answer to the question Why did I laugh? However, the Laugh Predictor 3000™ (in reverse gear) could only address the *perceptual* sense of this question. That is to say, it could only give information about my mindset as it responds to given formal, semantic, and referential aspects of the joke. This could help explain why I found the joke funny, in the sense that it could specify what it is *about me* that led to me finding the joke funny, rather than, say, distressing or boring (as others perhaps found it). Perhaps the Laugh Predictor 3000™ (in reverse gear) could highlight elements in the joke that had predictive value for my response. But it could not tell me *how* the joke was funny. That is, it could not offer the evaluative redescription that the aesthetic question demands.

The scientism of our age frequently leads to pronouncements that overstep the boundaries of their relevance. When applied to art and culture, the belief that "psychology lies behind it all" may be an alluring idea, but it is finally misleading because it ignores or denies the distinction between psychological and aesthetic explanations. One can see an outright collapsing of this distinction in an influential theory proposed by Thomas C. Veatch (1998) (and subsequently taken up as "benign violation theory" by Peter McGraw and Caleb Warren [2010], who set out to test it, with unconvincing results that they nonetheless lauded as proof. For example, given a scenario in which a man snorts his dead father's ashes, only 44 percent of those who reported seeing the behavior as a benign moral violation expressed amusement at the scenario, but the authors claim the experiment as proof "that benign moral violations tend to elicit laughter and amusement" [1]. One would surely expect at least 50 percent correlation to justify "tend to." "Tend not to" would be more accurate in this instance). Veatch begins by defining humor as "a certain psychological state which tends to produce laughter," before asserting that "humor and humor perception are the same" (162–63). This effectively asserts the redundancy of aesthetic explanations. In this formulation, humor is no longer an object of perception, much less an aesthetic practice, but instead the psychological state that attends the object. The object is effectively immaterial: it's all in the eye of the beholder. Veatch thereby collapses the question of what makes something funny (the properties of the laughable) into a question of why a particular type of person might be inclined to find something funny (the psychological conditions of a perception expressed in laughter). Veatch's theory is that humor "occurs" when "the perceiver views [a] situation as normal . . . and simultaneously as a moral violation" (164). It would seem to follow that the only good reasons one could give for one's laughter would be descriptions of one's own mood, inclinations, beliefs, values, and so forth—the conditions that gave rise to the perception. This ignores the fact that an account of personal history would not be an account of humor or even a justification for laughter. Veatch in his paper purports to be answering the question, What is humor? (193), but, more accurately, he is offering a hypothesis to the question Why would one person be inclined to laugh at something while another person (or the same person, later in life), faced with the same something, is not? He speculates, for example, as to why feminists (unlike sexist people) tend not to laugh at sexist jokes, why new mothers (unlike the childless) tend not to laugh at dead-baby jokes, why Minnesotans (unlike Californians) tend not to laugh at jokes that poke fun at Californians (although sadly no examples are offered). For Veatch, the incidence of humorous perception is dependent upon their "different subjective moral systems" (170), which determine whether they are capable of seeing a situation as simultaneously normal and as a violation. But whether or not this is sufficient to explain differential responses, it cannot justify Veatch's excursion into the realm of aesthetic diagnosis, for example, when he asserts that "some things are funnier than others . . . because more is better . . . if a joke is seen to contain several hidden violations, it will be funnier" (181). This is like saying that people who like ice cream tend to have a sweet tooth and concluding from this that the more sugar a brand of ice cream contains, the tastier it will be. If theory is to provide tools for the job, we must be clear about what the job is and what the tools are for. The mania for discovering the thing that pertains to *all* instances of humor seems to blind its advocates to the fact that this unifying feature will not—by definition, *could* not—distinguish between successful and less successful instances.

What "applying comic theory" typically means, in practice, then, is for a causal, motivational, functional, or perceptual hypotheses to lead a would-be aesthetic account. The analytical procedure typically takes the following form. First, a hypothesis about the basis of laughter is reverse engineered to construct a putative category of "the laughable." For example, if the cause of laughter is "a sudden relaxation of strain" (Dewey), then the laughable must be that which first creates strain and then induces relaxation. Or if laughter arises from a "conception of eminency" (Hobbes), then the laughable must be someone or something over which eminency is capable of being felt. Or if laughter is the expression of "the perception of the incongruity between a concept and the real objects which have been thought through it in some relation" (Schopenhauer), then the laughable must be this incongruity itself, the relation between a concept and some objects. A pic'n'mix approach, showing a pluralist willingness to consider how various theories may or may not apply, merely multiplies the problem. Whichever theory is chosen, the analytical procedure presents itself as a matter of finding, or inventing, ways to describe the comic instance in terms that align with this or that *a priori* conception.

The following part of the chapter illustrates the problem with this. Each section takes an influential theoretical statement in comic theory and seeks to apply it to a single sketch for which it would seem, on the surface, apposite. In other words, I have not sought to find "exceptions to a rule" by picking sketches that are evidently ill matched, but have instead aimed to suggest the limitations of using theories of laughter as a way of proceeding with an aesthetic account *even in the best possible case*. If the associated re-description is unsatisfactory even in *these* cases, then we should, I suggest, be skeptical of the analytical usefulness of what has tended to count as comic theory.

## Sudden Glory/"Swimming Pool"

> The passion of laughter is nothing else but sudden glory arising from some sudden conception of some eminency in ourselves, by comparison with the infirmity of others, or with our own formerly.
>
> —Thomas Hobbes (2010 [1650]: 65)

Figure 1.3. Lou (David Walliams) seeks the ear of the pool attendant (Steve Furst). Andy (Matt Lucas) prepares to dash. *Little Britain* (BBC, 2003–06, S1:E1).

Wheelchair-bound, bald, rotund Andy (Matt Lucas) and his mullet-wearing, goofy caregiver Lou (David Walliams) have arrived at their local swimming pool. Both are in their swimming trunks. Lou parks Andy beside the pool and heads off for a word with the attendant (Steve Furst). As soon as his back is turned, however, Andy takes off his eyeglasses, vaults out of his wheelchair, and mounts the steps of the diving board with unparalleled physical competence. This is all rather surprising. Meanwhile, Lou rambles on to the attendant about the help he may require given Andy's "slight fear of the water." He's so busy relaying this information that he fails to notice the enormous splash as Andy divebombs thirty feet into the pool below and begins to swim the length of the pool. By the time Lou has finished his monologue, Andy has clambered up the poolside ladder and reoccupied his wheelchair. At which point the unsuspecting Lou turns around to resume his place at its helm.

How useful is it to consider this sketch, from *Little Britain* (BBC, 2003–06, S1:E1), in the terms of Thomas Hobbes's account of laughter? In order to do this, would we need to draw from his statement, quoted above, a rough idea of the laughable. This is because, as suggested in the previous chapter, an aesthetic explanation cannot take the form of a mental report (e.g., "Here I felt eminent, and thus I laughed"). It needs rather to be a further description of the sketch itself. So, first, here is how we might derive an idea of the Hobbesian laughable from what is essentially (as claimed in the previous section) a perceptual account of laughter. Assuming that even "men who greedy of applause from every thing they do well" (65) are not capable of finding *everything* laughable (that is, not capable of finding themselves eminent over everything), we would expect the laughable to embody features that might plausibly foster "some sudden conception of some eminency." The term "eminency" is pretty broad, enough to cover a range stretching from smugness to triumph. At any rate, something must be there to suddenly produce or reaffirm conviction in one's own moral, physical, or intellectual superiority.

Superiority over what? The two forms given by Hobbes are superiority over others and superiority over one's former self, call it the recognition of self-betterment. In the first case, any comedic material that could be relied upon to provoke such a conception would presumably need not only to offer an instantiation of someone who is, in the words of Aristotle, "worse than the average" (quoted in Morreall, 1986: 14) but also to give some kind of prompt for the comparison of self and other. This might, for instance, conceivably take the form of a dramatic surrogate with whom we are led to identify and whose virtues can therefore be taken as akin to our own. In the second case, that of the recognition of self-betterment, Hobbes is principally thinking of jests, "the wit whereof always consisteth in the elegant discovering and conveying to our minds some absurdity" (65). Laughter at wit amounts, for Hobbes, to "the recommending of ourselves to our own good opinion" (65). In which case, the witty instance cannot be simply a clever reversal or a neat formulation, such as might lead to admiration for the other, but would need presumably to call upon our own powers of insight or intellect to give some basis for self-congratulation.

In terms of superiority over others, Lou's blinkered state and tendency to ramble would, on this account, represent the point of comparison for a conception of "eminency." In short, the joke is on Lou. The comic premise is not that disabled people are only faking it, but that a caregiver might fail to notice the first thing about the person he is supposedly assisting. Lou seems somehow to lack peripheral vision and basic auditory responsiveness; he doesn't catch sight of Andy and cannot hear the splash. This is understood not as physical deficiency, however, but as a character flaw, the consequence of his habitual fussing. Andy apparently knows he'll have the time to perform his feat and return to his wheelchair, which in turn allows us to surmise that Lou's blinkeredness is a constant and predictable feature of his behavior rather than a momentary lapse. It might further be seen as a moral flaw, in that his absorption in lecturing the pool attendant betrays an unseemly pleasure in conveying his responsibility as a caregiver. The patronizing way he approaches the pool attendant and sets about relaying what amounts to simple information in a prolonged, roundabout way, without allowing the monologue to become a dialogue, suggests an egotism in the guise of altruism. Ironically, Lou's inattentiveness is a consequence of being so busy virtue-signaling his attentiveness to Andy's (nonexistent) needs. It is Lou's self-image as "diligent" that compels him to convey his own sense of eminence over the pool attendant, whom he addresses as a servile fool. However, our perspective allows us to see that this self-image is poorly founded since Lou is easily duped by the savvy Andy, who knows that Lou is, in truth, a narcissist. Perhaps we congratulate ourselves for not being like Lou.

On this view, Andy would then be the dramatic surrogate with whom we associate ourselves. Again, the contrast between Lou and Andy is salient. While Lou is rambling on, using lots of words to say nothing ("getting him into the pool isn't really a kerfuffle, getting him out of the pool isn't really a kerfuffle, it's relatively kerfuffle-free"), Andy is the man of action, hurtling down the side of the pool, smoothly ascending the steps to the diving board. While the pusillanimous Lou worries about minimizing commotion (not wanting a "kerfuffle"—even the word is a timid euphemism), Andy fearlessly throws himself off the diving board, sets about making the biggest splash he can. His chief virtues are energy, bravery, and audacity. On the Hobbesian account, we might flatter ourselves that these virtues are our own.

However, the capacity to arouse eminency is not sufficient for a Hobbesian account. The feeling, or belief, that we are superior cannot arise gradually, dawning upon us by degrees, otherwise it would not compel laughter. The conception also needs to be brought about in an instant, in order for it to qualify as "sudden." The word is important enough for Hobbes to repeat it twice in his key phrase ("sudden glory arising from some sudden conception"). An aesthetic account of "sudden glory" would need to establish how something is both quick and surprising: accelerated tempo in combination with an unforeseen change of focus or direction. Three candidates present themselves as moments of "sudden glory": (1) the moment when Andy leaps from his wheelchair; (2) Andy's divebomb into the water; and (3) the point at which Lou turns back around, none the wiser.

The revelation in moment (1) that Andy is able-bodied is unanticipated by the first-time viewer. There are no hints that indicate that Andy is, in fact, able-bodied, and the news is not delivered in gradual stages but all at once. In his poolside charge, Andy does not show debility or confinement but muscular agility and freedom. Arise and walk (or, rather, run): a distant echo of the biblical miracle ("glory" indeed). Moreover, it is in this instant that the knowledge hierarchy opens up ("He's behind you": the refrain of the British pantomime). We can see what Lou cannot. Perhaps we take pleasure in the sheer fact of superior vantage, in the sudden disclosure of a secret.

With respect to the divebomb of (2), this is the visual and dramatic climax of the sketch. The gigantism of the splash might be felt to exemplify the phrase "sudden glory." Andy's impudence does not take the form of merely sneaking around behind Lou's back, a quick dip in the pool and then back in his chair. The divebomb is an audacious exhibition of liberty. Perhaps we share vicariously in its nose-thumbing glory.

Finally, in moment (3), the act of turning around and returning to the wheelchair is "sudden" in that the action is performed abruptly: Lou spins back round a mere beat after Andy has resumed his position. This is the instant we gather that this conspiracy will be successfully and forever maintained. It is also the point when Lou loses the last chance to overcome his ignorance, where even the evidence of Andy now being wet does not lead him to doubt. Perhaps we still harbored some residual belief that Lou would uncover the truth. This moment confirms him as a fool.

I think the above account, produced in good faith with the effort to derive a Hobbesian account of the sketch, is fine as far as it goes.

But it's not clear, on reflection, why the sheer fact of privileged access to Andy's secret should engender a feeling of "eminence," nor, for that matter, why Lou's gesture of turning around, although he does it swiftly, should be considered "sudden" since we anticipate it a mile off. These were terms given to us by the theory; hence, we felt duty-bound to include them. Being led by the theory leads to a kind of distortion in the resulting description. Moreover, I have to confess that I do not personally find myself, on reflection, tallying my own virtues, or savoring a feeling of intellectual or moral superiority, when I watch the sketch. All I can say is that "perhaps" *some people* watch it this way. But this is a very strange kind of claim. It is as if the theory lured us into offering baseless conjecture about what perceptions *might* arise for a suitably inclined viewer. Even setting this aside, the Hobbesian account is severely limited as an explanation of how the sketch is funny. This is as a direct result of its preoccupation with "eminence." Specifically, there are two crucial aspects of the sketch that an adherence to the superiority theory is liable to eclipse.

The first pertains to obscurity of motive. The above account postulated a viewer whose sense of eminence was produced through vicarious identification with Andy, against Lou. I therefore attributed to Andy an energetic rebellious spirit, along with a kind of savviness in respect of his calculation that Lou would not notice his excursion. Setting the theory aside, however, and with it the need to establish a basis for eminence, things start to look less clear-cut. What, after all, is Andy's *deal*? Since he can walk, why was he in the wheelchair in the first place? Why would someone dedicate his life to feigning a disability? Who would seek the privilege of being coddled and fussed over by a gasbag like Lou, day and night? Why would someone so clearly unable to resist the exercise of free will—compelled as he is, like a magnet, by the mere sight of a diving board—put himself in such a prison of dependency? Or, to put it another way, why would someone who was so utterly lazy as to prefer a servant to get him dressed in the morning now exert such energy, and for no other reason but a whim? And why would Andy, having put so much effort—over the course of weeks, months, perhaps years—into concealing his able-bodiedness now risk it all in such an extravagant and reckless manner for nothing more than a momentary douse—a pleasure he could enjoy every day if he but chose to give up his sham? Far from delivering us to a position of comfortable eminence, Andy's action of leaping from the chair unleashes a flurry of mad questions with no time for formulation.

The second crucial aspect of the sketch that an application of the superiority theory would neglect pertains to the marvel of its execution.

Perhaps the most glaring detail as yet unmentioned is that the sketch unfolds in a single, unbroken take composed in depth. The camera shows Lou and the pool attendant in the foreground while monitoring Andy's progress in the background, unobtrusively panning and tilting so that all three figures remain continuously visible. The superiority theory would struggle to explain why this is so vital, as it is, to the comic effect. The sketch would have been utterly spoiled if a choice had been made to intercut between the two activities.

One reason for the single-shot approach is that it emphasizes the coordination between the onscreen figures. Within the world of the sketch, Andy's poolside charge is improvised, and the timing of Lou's return is providential. But in the parallel unfolding world of the sketch's realization, we see that these have been choreographed. The long take allows for a vivid apprehension of this. For instance, Andy's leap into the pool is *timed* to coincide with Lou's declaration that Andy has a "slight fear of the water" and staged so that the splash materializes onscreen between Lou and the pool attendant. As an alternative to including it more peripherally in the frame, this makes the splash a more ostentatious contradiction of the claim and the nonreaction of Lou and the pool attendant more palpably absurd. Moreover, as if by some miracle, Andy hits the water *on the very instant* Lou says the word "water." Somehow,

Figure 1.4. Lou fusses in the foreground and Andy leaps in the far ground. *Little Britain* (BBC, 2003–2006, S1:E1).

the two syllables of "wa-ter," as fastidiously pronounced by Walliams, correspond precisely with the two-part entry-disturbance sound of the splash (bam-*tish*). The effect is a kind of duet, unifying foreground and background in a spectacle of synchronicity.

Another reason for the rightness of the long take is that it traces the whole of Matt Lucas's journey as Andy and hence verifies that the performer really is, by himself, undertaking this triathlon from start to finish. It matters, in this regard, that Lucas is by no means your typical athletic type. By documenting this feat—akin to the acrobatic routine of a circus clown—the sketch offers it for our appreciation. Moreover, the long take puts us in a position to observe that David Walliams prolongs his babble *just long enough* to allow Lucas to resume his place in the wheelchair—another accomplishment, since he is prevented from checking his partner's progress. It is essential that we understand that Walliams is feigning ignorance and, in fact, knows where his partner is. Yet it is this dimension of comic pleasure—the appreciation of performance, the recognition and appreciation of pretense—that is most starkly unavailable to the superiority theory, which can admit no distinction between a real and a simulated fool.

## Strained Expectation /"Monks' Humor"

> Laughter is an affection arising from the sudden transformation of a strained expectation into nothing.
>
> —Immanuel Kant, 1790 (2007: 133)

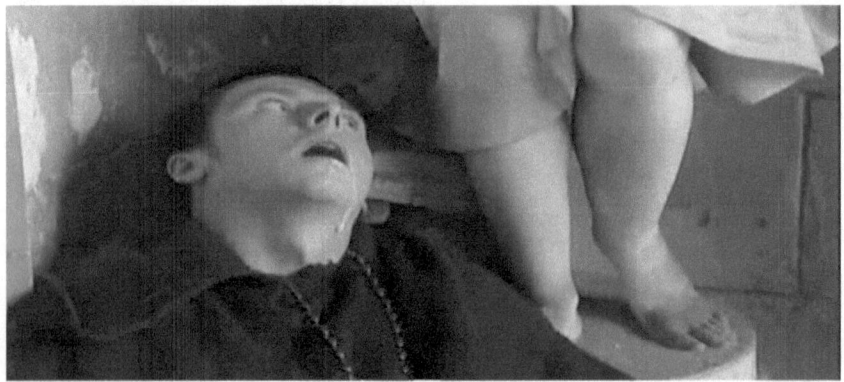

Figure 1.5. Simon Pegg is the petrified monk. *Big Train* (TalkBack Productions, 1998–2002, S1:E5).

The corpse of a young monk (Simon Pegg) lies slumped in a stone alcove, at the feet of a religious effigy. A close-up shows his eyes wide open and motionless, as if he has died in an experience of terror. A bead of white sputum dribbles from his open mouth. A church bell chimes. This is the arresting opening of a skit from *Big Train* (TalkBack Productions, 1998–2002, S1:E5), a surreal sketch show created by Irish writers Graham Linehan and Arthur Matthews.

Over the image of this corpse, we hear a voice booming offscreen—"*Demons*, Brother Dominic?"—and cut to a wider shot, composed in depth across the widescreen frame, that locates the victim center-frame between two further members of the monastic order. On the left, in the extreme foreground, is the speaker (Mark Heap), whom for ease of reference we shall call Brother Mark. On the right, in the middle distance, is Brother Dominic (Kevin Eldon), who listens anxiously, hands clasped before his cassock. Brother Mark lifts a Bible to his face, sniffs it, licks a finger, runs it over a page and tastes it. "Do demons use *poison*?" he continues, ominously. "I rather think our killer dwells somewhere CLOSER than the underworld."

We are evidently in the presence of some kind of hard-boiled Franciscan sleuth. (The immediate point of reference, for midnineties British viewers, at least, would have been a TV series called *Cadfael* [ITV, 1994–1998], based on a series of novels by Ellis Peters and featuring Derek Jacobi as a medieval mystery-solving monk.) Brother Mark gazes out of frame portentously, squinting as he muses on the sinister dealings that have lately visited the monastery. "DEATH follows these relics," he declares (what relics, we don't know). "Death . . . and—"

At this point, he is interrupted, however, as the "corpse" raises his head and issues a belly laugh in the direction of the would-be detective. Pegg's monk is not dead at all—it's all been an elaborate prank. Brother Dominic was clearly in on the joke, too, since the two of them fall about laughing together, roasting their victim, mimicking his voice, mocking his gullibility, even calling him a "twat." Moreover, to our surprise, given his previous grimness, Brother Mark takes this all in exemplary spirit. Rather than being cross with his fellow monks, he grins and shakes his head in relief and embarrassment. The elaborate composition of the shot is held, and the monks remain in their positions in the frame, but where previously this suggested fragmentation and distrust, the shot has now become a riot of joshing and teasing. For a surprisingly extended stretch of time, almost a minute, we watch the monks exuberantly celebrate the outcome in an excited and barely decipherable burble. End of sketch.

Of all the surprises for a first-time viewer of this sketch, perhaps the biggest surprise is the "long tail" that simply involves the three monks larking about, and nothing else. It's almost a kind of antijoke, the "joke" being that we remain with these characters for an extended period *after* the revelation, waiting for a punchline or subsequent reversal that never comes. In place of a further twist, the sketch offers the pleasure of watching three people continuously, and without strain, crack up, tease one another, laugh with one another, a spectacle of conviviality. It is extremely difficult to explain this to someone with whom it doesn't "connect." Perhaps, therefore, this might be an occasion to call on a theory of laughter.

The idea that humor involves surprise is common to many theories of humor but has a special place in Kant's formulation, with his statement that laughter is "an affection arising from the sudden transformation of a strained expectation into nothing." The statement offers an account of the experience of laughter or rather of the perception that gives rise to laughter. The phrase "strained expectation" is evocative and posits a forward-looking beholder who anticipates eagerly, almost desperately, a resolution to whatever problem is being set up. In the case of a verbal joke, we are presented with an impossible thought challenge that strains the imaginative capacity. For instance, the question What do you get if you cross a snowman and a vampire? is, if taken straight, that is, not as a joke, intolerably nonsensical. For one thing, it does not seem feasible that snowmen could be strategically interbred in the manner of show dogs, and certainly not with a wholly mythical creature such as a vampire. Perhaps we picture some kind of vampiric snow creature, with icy fangs, but this does not resolve the conundrum satisfactorily. In Kant's formulation, the punchline ("Frostbite"—aha!) relieves this (supposed) intellectual strain by removing the ostensible demand for a serious answer.

For an expectation to be transformed into "nothing," it cannot simply mean a state of expecting-no-longer (which naturally occurs whenever an expectation is either fulfilled or not). Nor can the expectation simply be left hanging, unresolved, since that is liable to lead not to laughter but to disappointment or frustration, as when we near the end of a gripping spy novel with hypotheses about what might happen, only to discover suddenly that the final pages have been torn out. So perhaps "nothing" in the context of Kant's remark should be taken to suggest triviality, that is, "nothing of consequence." We anticipate something monumental or meaningful, but, instead, we receive something trifling or nonsensical. We invested our attention in the anticipation of one kind of resolution—intellectual or dramatic—only to discover that nothing was at stake and that the premise lacked seriousness in the first place.

Working backwards from this perceptual account, one might therefore construct a picture of the laughable as a two-stage event, roughly corresponding, in the example of a verbal joke, to buildup and punchline. The first stage would stimulate an expectation and encourage an emotional or intellectual investment in the important premise or situation being presented. The second stage would effectively wrongfoot those expectations and dissolve that investment by presenting an outcome that renders the premise or situation a matter of no consequence.

To offer an account of the laughable in the "Monks' Humor" sketch in terms offered by Kant's definition of laughter would therefore entail an emphasis on the moment at which the "murdered" monk lifts his head and the pranksters burst out laughing. This would lead us to pinpoint this as the instant when our expectations of a murder case evaporate. Prior to this point, the sketch has deployed the iconography of Gothic horror to create a dark, suspenseful atmosphere: the harsh stone environment, the steady beat of a death knell, an innocent slaughtered in his prime. After the initial insert of the "murder victim," the scene is composed in dramatic depth-of-field with the corpse visible in the background throughout, Brother Dominic (potentially a suspect) lingering frame-right, and Brother Mark in close-up screen-left, earnestly trying to come to terms with this gruesome development. His words try to dispel a supernatural hypothesis for the murder, but his haunted stare, the mark of one who is no stranger to death, implies the presence of psychological demons, and his conspiratorial musings suggest an explanation no less sinister. To the extent that all this draws viewers into the mystery and invites them to anticipate further developments, it can be said to work in the service of a "strained expectation."

As for the collapse "into nothing," we could surely find no better candidate for the Kantian laughable than the revelation that this whole business has been an elaborate hoax. Should we laugh, our response may perhaps have taken a cue from that of the hoax's victim. Brother Mark's visible relief at the discovery, after all, takes the form of amusement, so perhaps we mirror his response. His laughing reaction confirms beyond question the harmlessness of the event and that it is not to be taken seriously. We understand the prankster monks will not be punished and that no further feelings of grievance will need to be exorcised. The revelation therefore precipitates no further chain of events and in this respect can perhaps be said to materialize "nothing of consequence."

This Kantian account immediately runs into trouble, however, since it seems to posit an infinitely credulous viewer who takes herself to be watching a mystery show rather than a work of comedy. Our hypothetical viewer would need to have stumbled across the sketch as an unanchored clip and to have taken it, and immediately invested in it, as a sequence in a medieval drama. She would need to take the elements of parody

Figure 1.6. From left to right: Mark Heap, Simon Pegg, Kevin Eldon. *Big Train* (TalkBack Productions, 1998–2002, S1:E5).

"straight," such as the contrived blocking of supporting figures in recess as the detective launches into sagacious monologue, and respond to, for instance, the white bead of sputum and the tolling of the bell as genuine dramatic elements rather than self-consciously invoking the conventions of Hammer horror. Our viewer would also need to be blind to the cues (or "comic twinkle" [Clayton 2012]) in Mark Heap's performance that place it as comic, such as his extensive eyebrow work, his out-of-frame squint, and his markedly ponderous delivery. Such features that engage a comic pleasure of recognition—specifically, a recognition of the conventions that construct "male wisdom"—would have to be left out of a Kantian account, with its requirement for a hopelessly naïve viewer.

Recognition is, on the contrary, essential to the comic effect, along with our *expectation* that a twist is forthcoming. In this sense, expectations are fulfilled, not dissolved. Given the presentation of Brother Mark as solemn and self-important, the comic principle that "pride comes before a fall" makes it abundantly likely that he will be undermined, even if the precise form of that undermining is not predictable. The victim lifting his head may come as a surprise to the first-time viewer, but *some* kind of rug pulling seemed inevitable.

Besides this, any aesthetic account seeking to engage Kant's hypothesis is liable to put all the emphasis on structure and to picture the sketch as a linear line of development. The moment of humor would, in this picture, be a single act of revelation, the instant when expectations are punctured, with everything prior to this moment working to build those expectations. The prototype for this theory is the verbal joke, with its conventional buildup/punchline structure. However, this presents a challenge for the articulated comic situation, such as we find in a sketch. Even in a skit as simple as "Monks' Humor," it is difficult to see how this picture of humor arising from a single sudden transformation could account for the way humor surfaces and resurfaces throughout. This quality is perhaps most marked in the extended shot of the monks celebrating, when the babble of excitement largely obscures the actual content of the exchange, occasionally clearing to allow us to hear an individual line, such as when Simon Pegg's monk says "I'm never heard him so serious . . ." or when Brother Dominic starts impersonating Brother Mark. These are not punchlines, exactly—more like ways of sustaining the festive mood.

Indeed, the turnaround effected by the midpoint revelation is best thought of as a dynamic shift in tone, rather than "the sudden transformation of a strained expectation into nothing." In an instant (and without the slightest camera adjustment), we move from the presentation of mutually suspicious individuals located in separate zones to the presentation of a laughing community joined from foreground to background. We are accustomed to seeing monks, and the institution they represent, as austere, reflective, sober, ascetic. At the moment of transformation, they morph into fun-loving jokesters, more akin to naughty schoolboys: there is no renunciation of pleasure in *this* monastery. Even with that, one might have expected Brother Mark to react haughtily or angrily to the prank. It would not, after all, in our world, be considered amusing—it would be considered outrageous, beyond the pale—to actually put someone through the distress of believing that his much-cherished friend has met an untimely death. Yet Brother Mark's reaction, when the hoax is revealed, is startling—and funny—for the lack of resentment he displays. Instead he generously takes it on the chin and even seems appreciative of the prank's execution. He is an *absurdly* good sport. This defies expectation, in a broad sense, yet the "transformation" itself is not the basis of humor and it does not result in "nothing." Instead we get a sustained scene of festivity, a glimpse of an alternative universe where anything may apparently be forgiven in the sacred name of merriment.

## Mechanical Inelasticity/"Awkward Conversation"

Any arrangement of acts and events is comic which gives us, in a single combination, the illusion of life and the distinct impression of a mechanical arrangement.

—Henri Bergson, 1901 (2005: 34)

Figure 1.7. Keegan-Michael Key and Jordan Peele (extras uncredited). *Key and Peele* (Comedy Central, 2012–15, S5:E5).

The most promising section of Bergson's *Laughter*, for someone seeking pointers for the analysis of sketch comedy, must surely be the second chapter, "The Comic Element in Situations." Unlike the other postulates we have so far considered, and unlike elsewhere in his essay, Bergson in this passage offers an aesthetic account of how humor is constructed, as distinct from a perceptual account of how it is received or a functional account of its social purpose. That makes it immediately wieldier than the other theorems thus far considered. By way of elaborating on his central thesis that comedy presents a "mechanization of life" (50), Bergson introduces three archetypes of comic construction that correspond to childhood pleasures. The first, the jack-in-the-box, describes a situation defined by a repetitious movement between containment and explosion, like the toy on a coiled spring whose operation alternates back and forth between being tensely held in place and then bursting forth when the lid is opened. The second, the dancing jack, is worked around a figure with the appearance of an autonomous individual but who is simultaneously shown to be the mere plaything of others, of higher forces or of inner drives: a living puppet moved by invisible wires. The third archetype Bergson calls the snowball, a situation marked by inexorable accumulation, where what started as a trivial matter accelerates into something large and out of control. While the imagery of a snowball might suggest something organic, Bergson takes it to exemplify the law of momentum, which is "mechanical" inasmuch as that the thing to which it applies moves unthinkingly, "by itself." Slightly undermining the neatness of the imagery, but nonetheless relevantly, he also adds that, like a machine (but unlike a snowball), comedy tends towards a characteristic of reversibility, often ending with a kind of reset or callback to where it began.

A textbook illustration of all these features may be provided by "Awkward Conversation," a sketch from the popular US television show *Key and Peele* (Comedy Central, 2012–15, S5:E5). Even more fittingly, allied to these characteristics is a satirical impulse to pick at social inflexibility and a certain quality of mindlessness. It's difficult to imagine a more amenable subject for a Bergson's theory. As before, I will offer an account of the sketch deploying the terms of its most amenable theory before reviewing what that account is liable to miss.

As befits a snowball structure, the sketch starts with something trivial and escalates quickly. A group of palpably nerdy students, sitting around a table in what appears to be the communal dining area of a college, are discussing comic book-to-movie adaptations. There appears to be a consensus of appreciation for Christopher Nolan's *Batman* series. That is, until one of the group members, a long-haired student played by Keegan-Michael Key, pipes up to say (in a close-up that visually isolates him from his peers) that, although he knows that he is in a minority, he finds these films overrated. A reverse angle shows the incredulous reaction of the rest of the group, favoring the smirking face of Jordan Peele, who is placed as gang leader. Shown in a tight three shot, he inclines his head in an arch manner towards his cronies and issues a sarcastic "O-kaaay . . ." Chief Nerd and the two remaining nerds, a hunched trio now shown in long shot arrayed along one side of the table, grin and snicker in communion, effectively cutting this dissenting voice out of their group. This action seems to rile Longhair, who retorts with visible irritation that he has merely stated an opinion and that's why he prefaced his comment with a qualification, that he knows full well it's a minority view. Early reticence having given way to indignation, we might identify this character as the Bergsonian figure of the jack-in-the-box. And indeed, Chief Nerd resolves to put him back in his box. We see him, in the very same tight three-shot as before, responding again by turning his head one quarter-left turn, and intoning, again with a sing-song tonality, an equivalently snide dismissal: "Awk-waaard." Here, in the guise of Chief Nerd, we have the figure of the dancing jack, whose appearance as the would-be witty opinion leader is marked instead by excessive gestural repetition, kneejerk irony, and a compulsion to please the group majority.

The jack-in-the-box leaps out again. "You know what? No. Not really," snaps Longhair, rounding on his sometime peer. "It's not awkward, at least not until *you* said 'Awkward.' *Now* it's awkward. Because of what *you* said." Once more, Chief Nerd performs a quarter-left head turn and another scoffing dismissal: "Any-waaay . . ."—this time embellished by some waggishly mobile eyebrows. But this time our jack-in-the-box will not stay in his box. "Anyway—what?" demands Longhair, pointing out in a hostile tone that "anyway" has to be followed up with an "actual contribution to the conversation." Again, the head turn: "Yikes" is the droll response. "No, look at me," our jack-in-the-box demands. "Look at me. Look at me. Look at me: there's no 'yikes.' And the reason there's no 'yikes' is that there's nothing scary about this situation." Longhair is now at the point of exasperation, marked by staccato hand gestures and head shakes. "Alll-right . . ." comes the wide-eyed reply from Chief Nerd, accompanied by the familiar rotation.

With each repetition, the snowball gains momentum. What started as a mere difference of opinion has now become a full-blown skirmish. Longhair now starts to underline every other word with a bang of the table. "All-right *what*? 'Cause after you say 'All-right' you *have* to *follow* that *up* with something." But his message is not getting through. Chief Nerd's head starts to turn, the cogs moving, this time as if in slow-motion, almost tauntingly, his eyes fixed on Longhair but his cranium drawn by an irresistible compulsion. "Don't do it," Longhair warns, with a stern finger. "Don't look at them. *Do not look at them.*" But no words can stop the snowball's inexorable motion. Chief Nerd pivots to his cronies, intoning, "Tell us how you *really* feel."

At this point, the snowball has reached critical mass. Words and gestures turn to action. Longhair grabs Chief Nerd's face and holds it firmly with both hands. "I really feel you're an asshole who has nothing interesting to say," he rants, eyes virtually popping in anger. Nerd tries to turn his head once more, but Longhair maintains his tight grip and strains to effect a counterrotation, so that Nerd is forced to face him directly with a glassy stunned look. Longhair issues a demand: "*Tell me* an opinion that you have about something. Just *one* opinion that you have about *anything* at all." Nerd's face trembles and contorts as if his brain were about to go into meltdown. But Longhair maintains his grip. "Share an opinion, share an opinion. Right now, off the top of your head. Just one opinion."

Imperceptibly, somehow, the jack-in-the-box and the dancing jack have switched sides. Now it is Longhair who is compelled to repeat himself ("Just one opinion, just one opinion"), the dancing jack driven by some inner mania. And Chief Nerd is now the jack-in-the-box, ready to spring, his face a seething mass of contracting muscles and eyes searching about in terror. Dissonant sounds build on the soundtrack in parodic evocation of the captive's mental turmoil. Finally, he erupts: "I-I-I *don't have* an

# The Trouble with Comic Theory 37

Figure 1.8. Heads will turn. Keegan-Michael Key and Jordan Peele. *Key and Peele* (Comedy Central, 2012–15, S5:E5).

opinion, that's why I just like what everyone else likes in pop culture!" The spring has sprung, and he's a jibbering wreck. Doleful strings now underscore the pathos of this revelation as his former friends squirm and shun their former leader. His shoulders become hunched, his hands curl into claws, and he shambles away from the table, crying, "Don't look at me!" The remaining group sits in silence, stunned by this display. Eventually, as if inevitably, Longhair yields to break the tension: "O-kaaay."

This final line performs a kind of reset in that the group has been reconstituted around the table and an ironic status quo restored. It also marks the completion of a process of transference whereby the dancing jack's one-time adversary seems to have been taken over by the very mannerisms he deplored. Indeed, the exact form of his sarcastic dismissal—"O-kaaay"—is a callback to the former Chief Nerd's first utterance in the sketch. Indeed, it is the first and only verbatim repetition of one of these dismissals, which have hitherto been variations to the same effect, which is why the closing line conveys such a feel of circularity or "here we go again." We might imagine the scene playing out all over again with a new victim, except with Longhair in the role of Chief Nerd.

The mechanical quality of Chief Nerd's behavior was not just a matter of vocal and gestural repetition; it was marked by a recurring formal treatment. In brief, every time he moves to address his cronies, the sketch cuts to an identical tight three shot of the "in-crowd" (excluding Longhair from the frame). This repeating cut is a match on action that effectively prolongs the head turning and centralizes the movement in the frame. This serves to prepare for the later emphasis on that gesture as a "telltale automatism," the betrayal, perhaps, of "some mechanism at work behind the living" (Bergson 23). Given that suggestion, Peele's facial shudders and spasms in the final part of the sketch, when Chief Nerd's head is held in place, deterred by force from its well-worn groove, might perhaps recall an android malfunction in the manner of John Hurt in *Alien* (Ridley Scott, 1979). Not only have we been given the impression that this particular character is incapable of shifting out of "sardonic mode," with its severely limited range of responses, but the fact that he speaks a recognizable script—a repertoire of lines favored by teenage clever dicks—implies a wider societal programming at work, a network of ironical androids.

The above account is offered as a Bergsonian "take" on what seems a quintessentially Bergsonian sketch. But, as with the previous case studies, there is some distortion that results from the application of the theory. For example, the metaphors of automatism, robots, programming, and so on that I have employed here are arguably prompted less by the sketch than by the framework with which I elected to describe it. There might be more exact, more salient, ways of describing its features beyond the recourse to mechanical imagery. Take, for instance, Chief Nerd's existential crisis when his face is gripped forcefully by Longhair. Warming to our theme, we were inclined to describe the trembling facial spasms as resembling an android malfunction. This is not a falsehood, but it is also not quite right. A fixation on the idea of "some mechanism at work behind the living" could, for instance, make us neglect the fact that at this juncture the scored music is more redolent of the war film than of science fiction. This helps frame the breakdown, albeit with a tone of parody, more as traumatic realization in the trenches than as a "does-not-compute" malfunction on a spaceship. The performance contains no twitching that would signal an electrical short circuit, for example. The most memorable characteristic of the tightly held face is one of pudgy cheeks that bunch as they are gripped. The flexible movement of skin over bones calls to mind the cranium beneath and the brain that fails to conjure its own thought. But there is nothing metallic to report in all this, and no hint of the digital glitch. And it's not clear that amplified robotic characteristics would have made the moment funnier.

An adherence to mechanical imagery might also obscure the way Chief Nerd's meltdown is marked by the appearance of animal characteristics. As he lollops away in retreat, curled fingers, bared teeth, and howls of anguish give the impression of a kind of teenage Quasimodo, shoulders hunched to shield him from the sight of others. He cries, "Don't look at me!," continuing the theme of looking and being looked at that became a preoccupation from the midpoint of the sketch as he continually looked away from Longhair. In this regard, the repeated slow head turn is a gesture of turning away as much as of a turning to be looked at. The two go together: affirmation is granted to he who flaunts his refusal to affirm the other. When Longhair forces Chief Nerd to *look at him*, he is simultaneously insisting on being recognized, refusing to be shunned, and denying Chief Nerd the superficial sustenance he obtains from being looked at by his peers. The pattern of looking and avoiding is completed when, in the final instance, having failed to come up with an independent opinion of any sort, his former minions avert their gaze and thereby deny him backup. At which point, Chief Nerd tells them *not* to look at him. Because the greater worry now is that they would see him for the miserable wretch he really is. Rather than mechanical qualities, we witness the emergence of feral qualities in Chief Nerd's demeanor. It is as if, without the approving gaze of others, without their superficial tokens of affirmation, he becomes an animal and must flee the social scene.

To see this craving for affirmation as a mere personality flaw, however, would be to miss the satirical bite of the sketch, particularly the point of the final line (Longhair's "O-kaaay"). For Longhair is *also* compelled to resort to sarcasm as a way of "clearing the air" or rather as a way of establishing his reign as Chief Longhair now that Chief Nerd has been

Figure 1.9. Shame. Jordan Peele. *Key and Peele* (Comedy Central, 2012–15, S5:E5).

banished. This is more than just a social tic; it is a way of policing the boundaries of the normal. Anyone found acting unusually, standing out from the crowd or defying group consensus, will be subject to this kind of dismissal. Irony is effective for this purpose because it declines to offer a sincere declaration of feeling or original thought that would be open, in turn, to challenge. To say "O-kaaay" is to perform a kind of shaming. It is an indirect way of declaring that someone has acted in some way excessively or has failed to operate according to the norms of the group, although without stating what those norms are, or why someone should be bound by them. Similarly, the phrase "Tell us how you *really* feel" is actually a way of saying "You have made an embarrassing spectacle of yourself by disclosing your inner convictions, when you should properly have been guarded about your feelings, like us." However, because it is coded, there is no way to deny this claim or challenge the underlying idea, at least not without continuing to disclose "how you *really* feel" and thereby opening oneself up for further rebuke.

The satiric target of the sketch, therefore, is not so much inelasticity as social cowardice. It suggests that this mode of discourse is governed not only by the fear of awkward silences and of unconventional opinions, but also by the fear of *not* being looked at and by the fear of being truly *seen*. Hence the plaintive music that accompanies the Nerd's existential crisis, forced to face his own vacuity in the absence of being able to muster an ironic deflection. Parodic as it may be, it suggests that behind the ironic mode of the smart-ass is a terror of finding oneself unoriginal, empty, with nothing to say. Hence the desperate need—not a mindless impulse but a survival strategy—to hold in abeyance, to ridicule and dismiss, even a modestly divergent opinion or the questioning of a turn of phrase, any intellectual act at all, anything that might reveal one's own flimsiness of values, for fear of the chasm beneath

## Conceptual Incongruity/"Sir Digby Chicken Caesar"

> The cause of laughter in every case is simply the sudden perception of the incongruity between a concept and the real objects which have been thought through it in some relation, and laughter itself is just the expression of this incongruity.
>
> —Arthur Schopenhauer (2000 [1883]: 76)

Schopenhauer's postulate is offered simultaneously as a perceptual theory (describing a way of seeing real objects that employs the lens of an ill-fitting concept) and as a causal hypothesis ("the cause of laughter": where a specific type of stimulus invariably, "in every case," gives rise to a spe-

Figure 1.10. The delusional Sir Digby (Robert Webb). *That Mitchell and Webb Look* (BBC, 2006, S1:E1).

cific manner of expression). To make it the basis of an aesthetic account of humor, one would need to assume that a text, image, performance, or whatever has been arranged in such a way as to invite the described type of perception, has not only presented the "real objects" but has also suggested the incongruous, unmatching "concept." (The alternative would be that the perceiver supplies the concept, in which case everything is potentially laughable—a merry thought, but not very useful for practical purposes.) Therefore, to apply Schopenhauer's postulate in order to account for the humor of a comic instance becomes a matter of specifying the nature of the mismatch between what has been presented and how it has been conceptually framed.

An example of a sketch that would seem eminently describable in those terms, "The Surprising Adventures of Sir Digby Chicken Caesar" appeared in the British sketch show *That Mitchell and Webb Look* (BBC, 2006, S1:E1). Perhaps best known for the Channel 4 sitcom *Peep Show* (Objective Productions, 2003–2015), comedy duo David Mitchell and Robert Webb could be said to make an unlikely, possibly "incongruous" pairing, since Mitchell's dominant comic persona is cerebral (bordering on pedantic), while Webb's is laid back (bordering on blasé). They play firmly against type, however, in this sketch, which features a neurotic, perpetually sozzled, down-and-out Digby (Webb), dressed in Victorian cape and deerstalker hat, and his hapless, equally drunken accomplice,

Ginger (Mitchell). In the brief episode I will discuss, Digby and Ginger collude to rob a man outside a pub. Summarized like that, it hardly sounds like promising material for a comedy sketch. But for those of us who find it funny, what is the source of our mirth? Might Schopenhauer's theory help explain it?

A Schopenhauerian analysis would seek to identify the humor as emerging from the relation between the "real objects"—the succession of misdemeanors—and the central "concept" of the sketch, namely, that Digby fancies himself some kind of secret agent and justifies all his actions in these terms. The contrast between ignoble behavior and moral vindication is made bolder by the sketch's use of a range of formal devices that align us with Sir Digby's subjective experience and put us inside his delusional and drunken state of mind. Instead of giving us an alternation between reality and fantasy, therefore, the sketch is constructed to allow us to see the former through the latter, to apprehend the depravity of Digby's world even as we entertain his fantasy that he is an undercover operative. Petty crime is framed as derring-do, cowardice badged as valor, desperation as the call of duty.

Incongruous conceptual framing is evident in the sordid heist that kicks off the sketch. As Sir Digby and Ginger plot to rob the customer at the pub table, their advance is accompanied by nondiegetic music providing some unfittingly grandiose suspense, a rising brass motif of the kind used to build tension in midcentury espionage thrillers, as if they were agents undertaking some intrepid task. The clash between chivalry and opportunism is heightened by the anachronism of the music relative to the modern-day setting and by the visual style of the sequence, which is largely composed of unflattering close-ups from body-mounted cameras and motion-blurred POV shots, both of which work to convey drunkenness. Having sneaked an unguarded wallet, Sir Digby grabs the man's keys from the table and hurls them into the street, yelling, "Stop thief! He's stolen your wallet, but he's dropped your keys!" As the victimized man heads off in pursuit, Sir Digby turns to his accomplice and shouts, "Quick, Ginger, we haven't a moment to lose!" On which cue, the pair set to work: downing the rest of the customer's pint, hoovering up his crisps, and puffing the rest of his cigarette. Meanwhile, on the soundtrack we hear Digby burbling a melody he presumably fancies as his personal theme tune, a slurred, drunken rendition of *The Devil's Gallop*, the inexpert, close-mic quality of which places it as Digby's "inner voice." Whether or not we recognize it as the theme from the British spy thriller series *Dick Barton—Special Agent* (Southern Television, 1979) or from some other cultural source that has appropriated it over the years, we can hardly fail to be struck by the mismatch between its connotations of valiant escapade against the patently undignified scramble presented by the image.

Finally, as the bandits make a getaway, we hear Sir Digby's interior commentary repurposing their exploits as moral crusade: "On a lonely planet spinning its way to damnation amid the fear and despair of a broken human race, who is left to fight for all that is good and pure and gets you smashed for under a fiver?" If this heroic framing is at odds with the dismal reality of the situation, two tramps fleeing the scene of a daylight robbery, the slippage in the final clause provides an additional conceptual incongruity, or turn of the screw. By continuing the line's momentum and completing its rhetorical triplet, the phrase "gets you smashed for under a fiver" is presented as a logical extension of "all that is good and pure." In Schopenhauer's terms, we might say that its humor derives from the notion of self-obliteration through alcohol being subsumed under the concept of pristine virtue.

This way of accounting for the sketch's first section is fine as far as it goes, but it barely touches on some of the most important elements in its realization. Adhering to the terms of the theory places an automatic stress on the intellectual contrasts of the sketch, when tonal and rhythmic factors might be just as significant. Picturing the sketch as a succession of sudden incongruities is liable to overlook, for example, the importance of pace. All that the Schopenhauerian conception would suggest, however, with regard to pace, is that the perception of incongruity needs to be "sudden." Clearly, we would need to say more. Pace is a function of how the situation unfolds in relation to how we are shown it, with music, editing, gestures, verbal delivery, and many other factors all playing a part. For example, when Digby gives the signal to Ginger to commence their feeding frenzy ("Quick Ginger! We haven't a moment to lose!"), the rhythm of the line (three syllables, followed by eight syllables in double time) forms a kind of musical anacrusis, or pickup, leading into *The Devil's Gallop*. The line stretches out like a plateau before the descent. The feeling of a launch is aided by the cut from an extreme close-up on Digby's face as he delivers the line, to a wider shot of the two men as they set about the table, timed to coincide with the start of the burbled musical theme. It gives an injection of energy, an acceleration that is crucial for the comic effect.

This acceleration, with its accompanying sense of mock grandiosity, is not wholly incompatible with Schopenhauer's notion of a "sudden perception of . . . incongruity." However, pace is very much secondary in that formulation. It asks us to understand laughter as principally arising from the intellectual juxtaposition between two features ("concept" and "object"). In its dualism, this risks neglecting the multitude of factors and features that are operative in the construction of humor. It also characterizes the apprehension of humor as a sober matter of spotting the relevant mismatch. This would struggle to account for the experience of disorderly delirium offered by the Sir Digby sketch.

Consider, for example, the sketch's use of body-mount cameras. With the camera attached to the performer's torso and pointed discomfortingly up into his face, the image achieves a queasy effect by reversing the usual figure-ground relationship. That is, when Sir Digby abruptly turns to his acquaintance, the camera moves with him, so he is the fixed point, relative to the lens, while the world spins behind him. This goes beyond delivering the information that the characters are drunk. It helps produce a *sensation* of giddiness akin to that of a fairground ride. It also contributes towards the broader dislocations of the sequence. No stable establishing shots assist the viewer's activity of trying to gather what is happening or where the characters are in relation to one another. The sketch opens with a blurry, handheld shot that moves fitfully around an indistinct figure at a pub table before swiftly jumping to an extreme close-up of a woozy-looking Sir Digby. Since these two shots are so brief and lack clear spatial matching, it is an immediate challenge to gather retrospectively that the first wobbly shot was a POV and to attribute it to the sozzled character (i.e., the usual triad of POV structure, subject-object-subject, is omitted). Similarly, when we see Digby nod to Ginger, but we don't know what he means with his nodding gesture. We can only reconstruct it as a signal to rob *after* they have made their way over to the customer and committed their crime. These challenges of comprehension, asking us perpetually to play catch-up, are not funny in themselves, but they all play a part in the sketch's strategy of disorientation on which its comic effect depends.

This is exemplified by the choice to introduce Sir Digby's "theme tune" in the midst of the heist, rather than prior to it, and to have it delivered by Robert Webb in a close-mic, deliberately amateurish way, rather than to have it played by an orchestra. In our attempt to account for the sketch's use of *The Devil's Gallop* in terms favorable to Schopenhauer, we ascribed a "mismatch between [the music's] connotations of valiant escapade against the undignified scramble presented by the image." But this is hardly the whole story and would be truer if the melody were rendered orchestrally rather than in this manner of vocal burbling, which is already at odds with "valiant escapade." The decision to have the tune suddenly voiced in this way is especially odd because the sketch started, hence could have continued, with orchestral music that we understood to be "internal diegetic." The change in instrumentation is thus a perplexing shift in aural viewpoint. With its studio lack of reverberation, the sound does not belong in the same outdoor space as the characters. Moreover, we hear the product of Robert Webb's lips at the same time as we see them fully occupied in draining the customer's pint glass. We have to find a way of reconciling it with the action, to surmise, for instance, that Digby is humming the tune to himself, narrating his own experience. We are thus simultaneously inside and outside his head. (What is the "real object" here? And what is the "concept"?)

Moreover, this interpretive demand from the soundtrack reaches us at the very instant the image explodes with action, as the tramps' frenzy of consumption is conveyed in an action-packed two shot: Digby puffing feverishly on a pilfered cigarette butt, Ginger licking the foil interior of a chip bag. The side-by-side staging makes them compete with each other for our attention, as well as with the soundtrack. The barrage of material continues as Webb's voiceover launches into its deranged interior commentary, rattling away with a pace we can barely keep up with and gesturing towards a cosmic perspective that is a further dislocation: "On a lonely planet spinning its way to damnation amid the fear and despair of a broken human race." Again, here, a surfeit in the image fights for our attention. The detail of Digby stubbing out the stolen cigarette and then promptly carrying away the glass ashtray, for example, like a souvenir from the crime, is almost missed amid the clamor. The makers of the sketch have taken the risk of a "pile-on" strategy, foregoing the opportunity to lay out each bit of business sequentially, a steady drip feed, and have instead elected to deliver *bursts* of comedic material, stacking up details, energizing them by making them almost fight with one another. And this, rather than an orderly parade of conceptual incongruities, is what gives the sketch its special thrill, soliciting that surge of exhilaration that, for shorthand, we call laughter.

## Against the Grand Reduction

The most common objections to theories of laughter are on grounds of universalism—namely, that no single theory can explain *all* instances of humor. However, in my view, that is already to concede too much, since it would imply that some instances *could* be satisfactorily explained in those terms. As this chapter has suggested, even when discussing instances that would seem maximally conducive to a particular theory, an account led by a laughter hypothesis tends towards distortion and the neglect of important elements of humor. This is largely to do with the attempt to use the wrong tools for the job: a theory purporting to explain laughter's social function or psychological basis, for instance, being inappropriately applied to the analysis of comedy. The tool-to-job mismatch problem is exacerbated, moreover, when the theory being applied encourages us to boil down humor to a single aspect. The trouble with comic theory is therefore not so much its claim to the universal as its inclination to the reductive.

To revisit a name from earlier in this chapter, Wittgenstein warns against the kind of explanation that takes the form: "This is only really this." In the notes from his seminars on aesthetics, Wittgenstein jokes about incinerating one of his students, named Redpath, before pointing at the remaining ashes and declaring, "This is all Redpath really is" (1966: 24). "Saying this might have a certain charm," he adds, cheekily, "but would be misleading to say the least." (24) Charm, for Wittgenstein, is always something of which we ought to be wary. Moreover, statements such as "This is only really this" have a double charm. There is the charm of elegance, offering a disarmingly simple solution to an ostensibly difficult problem ("only" this). And there is the charm of the exposé, claiming to reveal what *actually* lies behind misleading appearances ("really" this). Many prominent formulations in comic theory exemplify this tendency towards what I would call the grand reduction. Observe how Hobbes, for instance, declares the passion of laughter to be "*nothing else but* sudden glory" (2010 [1650]: 65, italics added), a phrase that conjures the image of a kind of theatrical unveiling. Likewise, Schopenhauer's grand reductive gesture is performed twice in one sentence when he asserts that the cause of laughter is "*simply* the sudden perception of . . . incongruity" and that laughter is "*just* the expression of this incongruity" (2000 [1883]: 76).

Bergson, too, appeals to the charm of simplicity when he writes that laughter is "*simply* the result of a mechanism" (2005 [1901]: 93). However, Bergson is less naturally given to reductivism, and you can hear his opposing inclinations fighting internally in the opening of his essay, when he follows up an initial round of scientistic questions ("what is the basal element in the comic? What method of distillation . . . ?," etc.) with an assurance that "we shall not aim at imprisoning the comic spirit within a definition" and that instead he wishes to strike up a "practical, intimate acquaintance" with comedy (1). Unfortunately, the mood does not last, and we soon find him resorting to such capitalized theorems as "THE ATTITUDES, GESTURES AND MOVEMENTS OF THE HUMAN BODY ARE LAUGHABLE IN EXACT PROPORTION AS THAT BODY REMINDS US OF A MERE MACHINE" (15), an equation that denies the contribution of any other factor in the achievement of the laughable (otherwise it could hardly be "in exact proportion"). Despite then briefly retreating from this reductivism, admitting that "it would be idle to attempt to derive every comic effect from one simple formula" (18), he subsequently undertakes the most impressive conceptual gymnastics in order to do just that.

Bergson was right on that passing point, at least. It *is* idle to derive every comic effect from one simple formula. Humor, I would like to say, is *irreducibly compound*. It will therefore most fruitfully yield to a form of analysis that is receptive to the multiplicity of factors in its construction and sensitive to the ways they meld and combine. The aim of this book is to demonstrate how that might be achieved, without the need for a guiding hypothesis—beyond the conviction, that is, that it is worth trying to say with some precision what it is that makes us laugh, to specify *how* something is funny.

# 2

# Takeoffs

## "Stayin' Alive"

THERE IS SURELY NO BETTER place to start exploring the "irreducibly compound" nature of humor than a celebrated scene from a movie frequently voted as the funniest of all time. *Airplane!* (1980) was written and directed by Jim Abrahams, David Zucker, and Jerry Zucker. Unlike that creative team's previous collaboration, *The Kentucky Fried Movie* (1977), *Airplane!* is not usually considered a sketch film. The film has a feature-length plot, lifted almost wholesale, along with large chunks of dialogue, from the strait-laced thriller *Zero Hour* (1959). This material gives much of the inspiration for gags lampooning Hollywood conventions. However, the storyline serves principally as the connective tissue for its succession of comic set pieces. The sense of overall narrative continuity disguises the extent to which the film is a collection of skits strung loosely, *lazzi*-style, along the thread of a disaster movie plot.

Despite its continuing popular appeal, the comic achievements of *Airplane!* have not been sufficiently acknowledged. Too often, the method is characterized, even by fans, as a kind of scattergun firing of cream pies at such a rapid rate that surely ("Shirley") some of them must stick. Such a view, while it rightly evokes the density of comic material in *Airplane!*, underestimates the deftness of its individual fragments. The example of comic brilliance I offer here is the flashback sequence that appears early in the film and features the Bee Gees song, "Stayin' Alive." Notionally offered as back story for how the film's central romantic couple became

Figure 2.1. Ted Striker (Robert Hays) struts his stuff in *Airplane!* (Jim Abrahams, David Zucker, and Jerry Zucker, 1980).

acquainted, the sequence is very much a standalone bit of business, a model of comedic craft and an exemplary piece of parody.

The scene is initiated by a ripple dissolve as ex-fighter pilot Ted Striker (Robert Hays) fondly recalls how he first met his (now ex-) girlfriend Elaine (Julie Hagerty). The location for this auspicious event is meticulously vague. Ted's voiceover relays how, when he was stationed "in Drambuie, off the Barbary Coast," he used to frequent the Magumba, "the seediest dive on the wharf, populated with every reject and cutthroat from Bombay to Calcutta," thus pinpointing its dockland setting in the general region of India, or Morocco, or Kenya, given the name of the bar, or perhaps Scotland, with its nod to brand of what may be the movie producer's favorite brand of whiskey. The satirical target here is the casual Orientalism of Hollywood, from which vantage most of the non-US world is simply an exotic elsewhere. But it is also a celebration of a mode of comedy where anything goes and nothing stays fixed for long. Over just a few seconds of screen time, the Magumba bar morphs before our eyes from being a wharf-side tavern (burly nautical types in beanie hats holding beer mugs) to a seedy strip club (the stockinged legs of a woman walking seductively along the bar to the sultry sounds of a trombone) to a hip jazz joint (the camera tilts up the body of the woman to reveal she is in fact *playing* the trombone). Over its course, and with no regard for consistency, the sketch will also absorb stereotypical aspects of the Western saloon (gambling and brawling), the small-town bar (jukebox attended by the town drunk), the underground gay club (sweaty barflies and prancing mustachioed men), the upmarket disco (fancy ceiling lights and dry ice), and the romantic ballroom (glitter ball and saccharine swing music). We have no idea where we are. The Magumba truly is all things to all people.

What is remarkable about these lurches in locale is how fluid the transitions are. The transfigurations are not exactly gags in themselves, but rather create a sense of perpetual volatility that fosters a mood conducive to laughter. A line of continuity creates a forward momentum that allows us to absorb these radical shifts. There is visual matching, for instance, when the voiceover declares, of the Magumba, that "you wouldn't walk in there unless you knew how to use your fists." On "walk" we see the footsteps of the trombonist across the bar; on "fists" we cut to a close-up of a hand laying out a royal flush—not exactly a fist, but it will become one soon enough when a fight breaks out. What would have been an abrupt leap to a new setup is bridged by the visual correspondence and audio overlay. The new gag also offers a variation on the preceding gag, where identity was revealed via a movement of the camera, so that it feels like a rhyme. Where previously the camera tilted up to reveal a stripper to be a trombonist, here the camera zooms out to reveal these gambling roughnecks to be a couple of pugnacious Girl Scouts. One brandishes a switchblade, and the other lands a punch and hurls aside the card table—each of these actions is matched to a trumpeted alert on the soundtrack.

The surprise of this reveal, the dramatic switch to high-octane action, and the dynamic way the shot adjusts from shallow focus to composition in depth as the rival Girl Scout is sent reeling from the punch, disguises a shift on the soundtrack. The commotion has engineered a shift from diegetic trombone to non-diegetic brass. The coordination between music and action is notable. Not for nothing is this film scored by Elmer Bernstein. The extended give-and-take of this brawl is elaborately Mickey Moused: one Girl Scout is thrown through balusters and crashes onto a table; the other has a beer glass smashed in her face and retaliates by swinging a chair into her rival's back—all the blows finding musical notation with a tone of high alert that suggests the vigilance required by a thriller.

Meanwhile, the barflies barely react, blithely chatting, drinking, and even clinking glasses as the place gets trashed around them. So, while the music plays up the histrionics, the body language of the extras suggests that it is perfectly usual to see Girl Scouts locked in mortal combat. What might sound like a simple incongruity (the idea that Girl Scouts would be the most ferocious types in a bar) is thereby ornamented so that it becomes difficult to discern what matches and what does not. The action is congruent with the setting (in the sense that fights break out in bars), but not with the types who perform it (in the sense that Girl Scouts are not your typical hoodlums). The music accords with the action (in the sense that it matches the drama of the fight) but is at odds with the reactions of the bystanders (who are, unlike the music, not the least disconcerted). Their blithe reactions are congruent with the setting (in the sense that the place has inured them to violence) but at odds with the action (in the sense that their proximity to the brawl puts them at risk of physical harm). Multiple sites of congruity and incongruity thereby jostle for our attention.

It may also dawn on us, with this extended exhibition of barroom violence, that the scene has lurched in a direction quite antithetical to the expectation of romance. How is the film going to make the seemingly impossible transition to a tender love scene, the promised first encounter between Ted and Elaine? It does so, remarkably, by setting off a line of virtual dominoes. One Girl Scout grabs the other by the pigtail and throws her along the bar. The punters all lift their drinks to accommodate the Scout's sliding progress, minding their own business, and when she shoots off the end of the bar, her head smashes into the barroom jukebox. This sets the machine off playing the lead-in to "Stayin' Alive," and this in turn sets the surly looking drunkard, who was leaning against the jukebox with an unpromisingly dour expression on his face, to start strutting in time to the music and moving his arms like a clockwork monkey. The camera pans with this social misfit as he swaggers over to a nearby disco arena and sensually strips off his jacket to join other grizzled types on the hitherto undisclosed dance floor—which is where our hero will see the girl of his dreams. As with the earlier connective strategy, the line of continuity smooths over the radical jumps in space and mood. There is even a shift in narrational tense, masked by the boldness of the cause-and-effect chain, from something like past continuous tense, a general illustration of the *sort of thing* that would tend to happen at the Magumba, into past historic tense, the narration of a *specific* event that is about to unfold: when Ted met Elaine.

A shot of Ted at the bar now shows his crisp white uniform tinted by the changing hues of the disco lights. This use of color is a neat device to sew together the spaces, while also casting Ted in a kind of disco haze that chimes with the rose-tinted nostalgia of his voiceover. It is wholly in keeping with the conventions of romance, of course, for the *mise-en-scène* of a flashback to match its narrator's mood. Against the background of this convention, however, the scene present details that contradict the

Figure 2.2. Ted (Robert Hays) must be dreaming. Barfly is uncredited. *Airplane!* (Jim Abrahams, David Zucker, and Jerry Zucker, 1980).

impression its ostensible narrator is trying to establish. Nothing in Ted's spoken account is expressly contradicted, and we understand the depicted events throughout the scene to be cued by his narration. Yet the flashback is flooded with details he would not or could not have recalled.

This is to identify a problem associated with the convention of the first-person flashback in general, namely, that pictures always show more than words can say and more than any memory could elicit. But here the problem is needled for comedic purposes. Ted recollects, for instance, in the voiceover, that he was so entranced by the sight of Elaine on the dance floor that he had to ask the guy next to him at the bar to pinch him, to give him the assurance that he wasn't dreaming. The music drowns out the dialogue between them, but we see Ted leaning in and speaking to the stranger on his left. What the voiceover fails to mention is something we can too plainly see, that the guy next to Ted at the bar is a burly sailor type with tattoos and sweat stains. Visibly unnerved by the proposition of pinching, the sailor makes a hasty exit, screen right (unseen by Ted, whose gaze remains fixated on Elaine). This broad gag depends upon the spoken narration to set up the context for the misunderstanding since otherwise we could not guess what Ted was whispering into the sailor's ear. Yet the humor here is only partly a matter of what Arthur Koestler calls "bisociation," "the perceiving of a situation or idea . . . in two self-consistent but habitually incompatible frames of reference"—that is, pinching is associated simultaneously with being woken from a dream and with flirtation or with heterosexual infatuation and homosexual invitation (1964: 35). It would have been an option to show Ted realize, only too late, how his words might have been taken the wrong way. This would have left bisociation intact, yet the comic effect would have been wrecked, because it would then seem as if Ted were narrating this faux pas. Ted's failure to recognize, both in the moment and thereafter, how his request has been misconstrued by the burly sailor mobilizes a flashback paradox. If he failed to see it then, he could hardly recall it later. This introduces the odd notion that the flashback is somehow being shaped by two competing narrational agents: one earnestly relaying and embellishing a romantic episode and the other mischievously reframing and undermining that account at every turn.

This is a crucial dimension of parody, overlooked in the theoretical literature on the topic, which tends to emphasize referentiality and "trans-contextualization" (Hutcheon, 2000: 15). What we are invited to entertain in parody is the idea of a straight or generically faithful chronicle that is continually being upset or undermined as if by an impish saboteur. The "saboteur" narrator introduces details and ways of seeing that are deliberately at odds with the efforts of the "official" narration. Both narrational agents are textual effects, of course, but the effect is to stage a kind of metafictional tussle between a pair of puppet narrators.

We sense a kind of sabotage in our sequence, for example, in the sporadic callbacks to the hyperbolic skid-row milieu with which the "official" narration began but which it now wishes to suppress in favor of glamor and intimacy. On the disco floor, we see Elaine gaily mirroring the moves of a dance partner. "I was afraid to approach her," Ted's voiceover relays, "But that night, fate was on my side." While Elaine is momentarily turned away from her partner, the fellow has a knife stuck in his back by a nearby miscreant, and on spinning back to face him, Elaine continues mirroring his agonized contortions, as if he were teaching her the latest moves. As always, it's the little details of execution that make for funniness—the way the assailant accompanies the stabbing action with a chic, Travoltaesque, flourish of his spare hand, and then just carries on dancing, brazen as you like. This random act of violence conveniently clears a path for Ted's advance, pricking his narration by suggesting callous opportunism where the voiceover had invoked the benign hand of fate. Similarly, later on in the sequence, when Ted and Elaine throw some shapes, seeming almost to float on the disco clouds produced by a fog machine, there is an inserted callback to our ferocious Girl Scouts that irrelevantly contaminates the otherwise dreamy atmosphere. The camera pans away from Elaine, across the crowd of revelers, and finds these savage girls, hands gripped around one another's necks, still locked in a battle to the death in the depths of the disco smoke. It's as if our saboteur narrator went looking for something to scuttle the amorous mood.

The dance between Ted and Elaine is, of course, a spoof of *Saturday Night Fever* (1977), memories of which would have been fresh when *Airplane!* was released in 1980. Allusions include the mirroring of moves between dance partners (as between Elaine and the stabbing victim), the idea of the candy-colored dance floor as theatrical stage (as when Ted starts performing Ukrainian squat kicks for the admiring crowd; someone even hurls in some juggling balls, and the thing goes full State Circus), plus the gyrating camera that takes on the point of view of a spinning dance partner (deployed when the waiflike Elaine, defying the laws of physics, takes the legs of her strapping partner around her waist and whirls him around and around). Most striking of all is the white three-piece suit worn by Robert Hays as Ted, directly recalling the outfit (ivory vest over black shirt) famously sported by John Travolta.

Pleasures of recognition aside, the opportunity is taken to perform a sort of male burlesque. This starts with Ted's approach to the dance floor, first circling around Elaine, then removing his white jacket, swinging it around his head and releasing it with élan into the crowd, before striking the famous Travolta sky-pointing pose. As soon as he has assumed this position, however, the jacket is flung back from offscreen, presumably in anger, returning the debris of his love-making. To his credit, Ted commits to holding the pose as the crumpled jacket slides down his torso.

Figure 2.3. Ted (Robert Hays) busts some serious moves. *Airplane!* (Jim Abrahams, David Zucker, and Jerry Zucker, 1980).

When he strikes the sky-pointing position again, later in this pageant, the decision is taken to overbake, rather than to undermine, his show of virility. This time, when he jabs in the air, we hear a cowboy pistol ricochet and a collective, almost orgasmic, gasp from the onlookers as they respond to this manly display. It makes us wonder what Travolta's move was meant to suggest in the first place, with that finger that points at nothing: the peacockish gunslinger, urban warrior, firing invisible bullets and offering his body as a sexual totem.

This gunshot is the latest in a succession of sound effects that Mickey Mouse Ted's movements. Each is an ostentatious addition, blatantly nonorganic to the scene, that can be heard as an impertinent comment on the action. Ted has lately returned to the dance floor after briefly being flung some distance by Elaine's whirling action. When she lets go of his legs, the centrifugal energy carries him up and away, with a cartoon *whooosh*. He sails through the air with surprising grace, even performing a somersault, but then his unseen landing offstage is accompanied by an extravagant *crash-hhh*. Leaping back onto the dance floor, his visually balletic return is made mechanical by the *dugga-dugga-dugga* sound of an oscillating springboard. The saboteur narrator has taken control of the sound mixer.

The springboard sound offers a variation on the sequence's key motif. Ted's dynamic reappearance on the dance floor, after having flown through the air and briefly vanished from our sight, caps a series of what might be called boomerang gags. Some of these have been discussed already:

1. Advancing toward Elaine on the dance floor, the impetuous Ted flings his air force cap out of frame (with a cartoon *wheeee*); he exits the frame, and the cap flies back, striking the barman who is busy collecting a tip.

2. Ted, on the dance floor, tosses his jacket out of frame; he strikes a pose, and the jacket comes back, hitting his body.

3. Ted spins Elaine around, throws her up and out of frame; we watch him ready himself, for an amount of time that suggests she attained an extraordinary height, before catching her.

4. Elaine spins Ted around, and accidentally lets go so that he flies through the air and out of sight; but then he leaps back onto the floor.

Each of these moments, in its own way, involves the motif of throw and return. Once the pattern has been instituted, each of these gags becomes a variation on a theme, and thus each, in its way, is also a kind of return. This can be extended, moreover, to the various callbacks in the second half of the sequence, such as the distinctive barroom drunkard who reappears in the crowd, performing a boogie in an insert shot as Ted and Elaine strut their stuff, and those truculent Girl Scouts, one of whom we last saw being hurled in the opposite direction to the dance floor (and perhaps we figured that was the end of her). There is also the recurrence of movements: twice we see partners mirroring one another's moves, twice we have spinning, twice we have the sky-pointing pose. More abstractly, there is the perpetual restitution of the "official" chronicle, no matter how many times it is thrown off course by the "saboteur" narration. There is more to this boomerang pattern than the pleasure of formal variation. It gives the sequence as a whole a feeling of buoyancy that exemplifies something about comedy more generally. If the uncanny is the monstrous return of the repressed, comedy is something like its opposite: the joyous return of the irrepressible.

## "Acorn Antiques"

The textual mimicry involved in parody need not take the form of a lampoon. Indeed, a given parody's relation to its notional textual "targets," or to the genre it apes, may just as well be as affectionate as critical. It

Figure 2.4. Miss Babs (Celia Imrie) answers the phone at Acorn Antiques. *Victoria Wood: As Seen on TV* (BBC, 1985–87, S2:E3).

may be even be relatively unimportant, in some instances, whether the viewer is able to recognize what, if any, *specific* texts are being invoked. There are aspects of the appeal of parody beyond the acerbic bite of satire and the satisfied glow of recognition. There are, most notably, pleasures involved in the play of intentionality made available by the project of doing something badly *on purpose*.

A case in point would be "Acorn Antiques," a series of sketches that appeared as part of the BBC show *Victoria Wood: As Seen on TV* (BBC, 1985–1987) as a fond send-up of a contemporary, now largely forgotten, soap opera. British viewers in the mid-1980s would have recognized "Acorn Antiques" as a pastiche of the long-running serial *Crossroads* (ATV, 1964–1988), with its dreary opening credits, languid theme tune, creaky sets, misjudged emphases, and half-hearted commitment to continuity. Some specific storylines and characters are invoked: *Crossroads*'s stoical housekeeper, Mavis Hooper (Charmain Eyre), for instance, is caricatured by Julie Walters in her role as the tea lady, Mrs. Overall, a hunched figure reconciled to her own servility, as the name too aptly suggests. More important to "Acorn Antiques" than these specific references, however, is its recall to the days (predating the production of this sketch) when soap operas were routinely recorded live, on a shoestring budget, with multiple camera feeds mixed live for imminent broadcast. We don't really need to have specific knowledge of such programs; we just need to imagine we are watching one, with its manifest production bungles, fluffed lines, and missed cues.

The imagined demands of live production are what give "Acorn Antiques" its distinctively skittish tone. The rolling camera magnifies every gaffe. Under-rehearsed actors struggle to wrap their tongues around clunky dialogue, highlighting the flaws of the script, and find themselves malcoordinated both with the labors of camera technicians and with the whims of the vision mixer. Those who find themselves in the wrong spot are left to squirm it out. The perpetual requirement to move on, to the next line, to the next scene, offers no chance for redemption. Everyone is on edge.

This antsy feel is exemplified by an early shot in the ninth installment of the sketch, "Drastic Refurbishment" (S2:E3). The function is to establish the locale and show the arrival of one of the main characters. The coiffured diegetic actor (played by Celia Imrie) who incarnates the storeowner Miss Babs needs to step out of a van and walk to the door of the eponymous antiques dealership. The camera operator needs simply to pan with her movement and tilt up to the store's sign. But problems arise. One issue derives from the unfortunate fact that Miss Babs has been given a squat porcelain vase to hold for this scene. We gather that someone, perhaps the fictional director, has decided this would be an apt prop to convey the character's everyday role as an antiques dealer. She also carries a handbag and gloves, presumably to convey the information that she is also a metropolitan sophisticate. Unfortunately, this collection of props makes her exit from the vehicle more awkward than it needed to be since in order to close the van door, she needs to clasp the gloves, bag, and vase in a single clawed hand. The sight of Miss Babs casually juggling an unwrapped vase, which has apparently been stowed on the passenger seat, undermines the idea that the object is in any way precious. Perhaps she is blasé or else a merchant of worthless junk. Either implication seems counter to the "intended" effect.

Further production issues manifest as Miss Babs strides toward the shop door. There is, in fact, a bunching of little (deliberate) mistakes. Just as she is about to reach the doorway, our actor briefly stumbles as one of her high heels loses contact with the paving slabs. At the very same moment, a couple of figures are made visible in the shop window and abruptly and conspicuously shuffle out of view in an ungainly effort to rescue the shot. (We might recognize them as Julie Walters and Victoria Wood, in costume.) Furthermore, with a haste that suggests a reactive attempt to crop these loitering actors out of frame, the diegetic camera operator performs a clumsy tilt and half-baked zoom to the store sign, which consists of stick-on letters carelessly pasted and misspelling the name of the venue: "ACORN ANTIQES." This array of "blunders" (prop malfunction, performance slipup, production blooper, camera swerve, décor howler) is arranged as a cluster. Staging them in quick succession means that our eyes must dart across the screen: down to the flattened heel, up to Imrie's reaction, over to Walters and Wood ducking out of sight, before our gaze is "averted" by the camera's yank, upward to the misspelled sign. None of them is afforded the articulation of an independent gag; cumulatively, they convey something like a plague of miscalculation.

It is in the nature of an antiques shop for it to be filled with incongruously related items divorced from the functions and contexts that once gave them sense as objects. The sketch takes advantage of this fact when it moves to the interior. The décor seems to have been arranged to deter our eye from settling on any single focal point. The frame is crowded with curious knick-knacks and bizarrely ornate objects that direct focus away from the human figures that are supposed to compel our attention. As the camera drifts sideways to follow the movements of a couple of browsing customers, and to bring into frame Miss Babs's office nook, our attention is likely to be distracted a life-size ceramic leopard that sits beside her desk with a perpetual snarl and by the shiny, rather hideous, swan-shaped vase that protrudes into frame as the camera settles on Miss

Babs, who wears a look of concentration and has a telephone receiver pressed to her ear, apparently waiting for the camera to get into position before delivering her salutation (long pause . . . "Hello, Acorn Antiques, can I help you?"). The construction principle of this sketch is to pepper the scene with distracting details, forming a kind of compositional jumble, as if to evoke the invisible fog clouding the judgment and ability of everyone who works on this diegetic soap opera. No member of its crew has pointed out, for instance, that listening intently to the receiver for five seconds *before* delivering a welcome message is a profoundly odd and unnatural way of answering the telephone.

This compositional strategy allows for certain comic elements to dawn upon us, gradually, having been hidden in plain sight. We may not notice, at first, the movement in the background of the shop as Miss Babs speaks on the telephone and to recognize it as a white mug being repeatedly lifted up and returned to a tray, as the actor playing Mrs. Overall (played in turn by Julie Walters) waits in an accidentally visible offstage area to make her scheduled entrance. The shot is cleverly composed to make this detail available without making it leap out, with so much else to command our attention. The choice of a white mug initially camouflages it among other white objects (including the swan) and aspects of décor (white railing and a white pillar). Only when it moves up and down (the actor taking a sip while she waits!—why not?) might it draw the eye to the background right of the shot. And even here it competes with other "mistakes" and self-contradictions in the foreground, such as the mime gesture Imrie performs—sticking her finger in her ear—as she asks the person on the end of the line to speak up. The shop is supposedly noisy because they are undergoing "extensive alterations and drastic refurbishments," quite against the evidence of the soundtrack. It seems somebody forgot to add sound effects. As for the extensiveness of the alterations, Miss Babs assures the inquirer that they are "sticking with mauve": refurbishment isn't *that* drastic, then. The fact that someone has been visibly waiting "in the wings" all this time might come to our notice at any point during the unfolding of the scene. It only demands our attention when Miss Babs reports to her telephone interlocutor that "Mrs. Overall is standing over me with a cup of coffee." With that line, we gather that the actor playing Mrs. Overall has entirely missed her cue. At which point, she hastily returns the mug to the tray and lurches into the scene.

The perceptual demands of this early part of the sketch are followed, in the ensuing dialogue between Miss Babs and Mrs. Overall, by the mental demands of following a mesmerizing chain of nonsequiturs. The delirious script—worthy of the Marx Brothers—runs as follows:

OVERALL: I've been standing here so long this coffee's practically congealified.

BABS: Oh, Mrs. O., nobody would think you had a degree in linguistics and advanced semantics.

OVERALL: Well, I had to do something while I was recovering from that transplant.

BABS: Yes, we were grateful for you donating all that bone marrow to Miss Berta.

OVERALL: I hope she got it all right.

BABS: I'm afraid some of it had leaked out of the jiffy bag.

OVERALL: [tuts] Men!

BABS: Yes, the doctors are very pleased with her.

[Pause]

OVERALL: I heard she might never play the gramophone again.

The editing of this exchange offers an anticipatory alternation between one-shots of each speaker as each delivers her dialogue. This parceling out exacerbates the staginess of the scene, while highlighting the tenuous, occasionally unfathomable, connection between consecutive lines. The onus is on the viewer to try to reconstruct the crazed rationale, or deduce the manner of oversight, that led to the mangled dialogue. For example, when Miss Babs refers to Mrs. Overall's degree in linguistics and advanced semantics, we might gather that this line is a comment on her use of the word "congealified." But then what might otherwise seem like a quip is developed as genuine backstory: "I had to do something while I was recovering from that transplant," Mrs. Overall remarks. The implausibilities pile up. We are asked, first, to entertain the idea that a degree in linguistics and advanced semantics might be undertaken simply to pass the time during hospital recovery. Then we have to imagine that bone marrow can be self-extracted, and, what's more, hygienically stored and transported in a padded envelope. Finally, we are asked to accept that Mrs. Overall had not previously inquired, during all the time it took her to recover (enough time to pass her degree), whether

her intended recipient had even received the donation ("I hope she got it all right"). In parallel to all that, there is in play here an idea about class-based servitude, the extremity of Mrs. Overall's selflessness being meanly repaid by uneffusive acknowledgment from her employer. "*All that bone marrow*" is a glorious touch, conjuring the gruesome image of dear Mrs. O not just scooping out a teaspoon full, but excavating great heaps of her precious interior jelly. An act of volunteerism well beyond the call of duty, rewarded by the meagre "we *were* grateful."

The credibility shortfall in this scenario we can attribute metadiegetically to some complacent team of scriptwriting hacks, devising this backstory perhaps as a way of explaining an actor's temporary departure from the cast. However, the rationale for the next three lines, as quoted above, a superlative sequence of nonsequiturs, is beyond reconstruction. Nothing, no reference to a particular man or group of men, seems to prompt Mrs. Overall's cursing of the masculine sex ("Men!"). After a pause, Miss Babs seems to respond to an unheard query by confirming Miss Berta's strength of recovery ("Yes, the doctors are very pleased with her"). This seems to suggest that the actor playing Mrs. Overall missed the cue for her previous line, and the actor playing Miss Babs just carried on regardless, hoping the audience wouldn't notice. The missed line would need to have been something that would have warranted the affirmative reply, such as, "I hear Miss Berta is doing well." But the following line seems to contradict this rationale since it laments, via a bizarre rumor, the degree to which Miss Berta has been maimed: "I heard she might never play the gramophone again." Perhaps we can assume, here, that the actor bungled the line's key noun, and was supposed to say something like "saxophone" or "xylophone." Even then, the claim is distinctly odd and out of place in the sequence of lines. We seem therefore to be faced with the results of slapdashery on at least three counts: dialogue that has been poorly conceived *and* further garbled by the actor *and* delivered at the wrong moment—the collision of which makes whatever sense was originally intended impossible to discern. This kind of thing is what makes the sketch so comically exhilarating.

Getting things back to front and out of order is a familiar pattern of "Acorn Antiques," and the sketch offers a succession of preemption gags. Miss Babs declares that she hears the postman before there is any audible trace of him. As there seems to be a delay, she fills the awkward silence with her next line: "That looks like an important letter." Only *then* does the anonymous extra playing the postman act out his delivery task by flinging an envelope round the side of the door. Miss Babs volunteers to retrieve the letter but then sits back down and says, "Oh, you're too quick for me"—before the hunched Mrs. Overall has even started to haul her weary bones to retrieve it. The outbreak of missing cues is made worse by the way the actor playing Miss Babs insists on sticking rigidly to script. When Mrs. Overall declares that the letter is Miss Babs's "Decree Nisi" (a court order for a divorce), she pronounces the Latin word accurately with a long "i" ("Nigh-sigh"). Miss Babs then takes it upon herself to correct Mrs. Overall's pronunciation ("Nisi, Mrs. O") but pronounces it exactly the same way. In response to which, Mrs. O berates herself: "Nisi, I always get that word wrong." The exchange is initially baffling until we deduce that the actor playing Mrs. Overall was supposed to *mis*pronounce the word "Nisi" but accidentally pronounced it correctly, and the actor playing Miss Babs, incapable of improvisation, failed to correct her own line of correction. It would take a degree in linguistics and advanced semantics to get to the bottom of *that* irony.

As the above discussion illustrates, "Acorn Antiques" is challenging to describe for the same reason that its humor is complex, because it engages the simultaneous perception of three diegetic "levels." Each onscreen figure is a soap opera character, a fictional actor, and a comic performer. Each of these aspects is foremost at different points, but they are concurrently available throughout—the latter most prominently in the occasional moments when its performers laugh, that is, fail to maintain a straight face, which are kept in the sketch, as if to embrace the genuine flub in the midst of countless faux flubs. Our awareness of the constructedness of the soap opera, with its wobbly set and insecure

Figure 2.5. The marvelous Mrs. Overall (Julie Walters). *Victoria Wood: As Seen on TV* (BBC, 1985–87, S2:E3).

actors, is accompanied by an apprehension of the constructedness of the sketch. We imagine what fun it must have been to put this material together. When Miss Babs asks Mrs. Overall whether she believes "the triplets" are really hers ("after all I did only go into hospital to have my ears pierced"), she takes the envelope in hand and stands up behind her desk, briefly gazing out of frame before returning to look at Mrs. Overall with a furrowed brow. We recognize the gazing out of frame and the melodramatic standing to ponder as conveying the pensiveness of the soap opera character *and* as crummy acting on the part of the fictional actor *and* as a set of soap opera clichés knowingly invoked by the comic performer. When we now cut to a new angle in anticipation of Mrs. Overall's reply, we discover that Julie Walters's face is, in the reverse angle, obscured by the envelope that Imrie is holding. On the diegetic level, this is a production gaffe, the consequence of an actor taking insufficient account of the position of the second camera. But on the level of comic performance, this "mistake" is carefully choreographed, a matter of Imrie hitting a precise mark to block the cross-shot of Julie Walters.

The camera accordingly jerks upward to allow a clear view of the actor's face. This, too, is a gesture understood on two levels at once: at the diegetic level, the fictional camera operator reacts to the blunder with an impromptu and overcompensating pedestal adjustment; at the level of the sketch, the sudden lift of the camera gives special emphasis to Walters's final line. The camera movement is in fact timed to coincide with the preparatory words ("Put it this way . . .") to create the effect of kind of grand lead-in: "Put it this way," she says, the camera rising to absorb her wise words, "you can't break an omelet without beating eggs." Then, realizing in alarm that the expression didn't come out right, she tries again. "*Eating* eggs." That's not right either, but time has run out. The two ladies remain standing for the end-of-scene tableau and a melancholy piano rendition of the theme tune.

The crush of thoughts provoked by this word stew includes the dim recognition that *break* rhymes with *make* and that perhaps the actor, in her panic, has replaced the wrong verb with its rhyming counterpart ("eating" for "beating" instead of "make" for "break")—except, of course, that "You can't make an omelet without *beating* eggs," while a true statement, is not quite the adage either. This sets off a kind of contagion of muddlement in ourselves as we struggle, in the stupor of the moment, to recall the *actual* expression, puzzle at how it has gotten so mangled, and wonder what its relevance would have been to the prior dialogue even if it had been correctly uttered. So what we have is a bungled rescue of a botched delivery of a misplaced line. The specter of meaninglessness, as well as the stench of failure, hangs in the air during the formal pause that ends the scene. The theme tune jingle that caps the exchange becomes thereby a kind of ironic lament, a hilarious expression of disappointment. Trying to put things right just makes things worse. Still, you can't break an omelet without eating eggs.

## "Spiffington Manse"

Comedy is often associated with excess. But how much is too much? Perhaps, if we accept that "too-much-ness" is part of the fabric of comedy—typified, as it is, by formal repetition and the frequent contravention of norms—the question should be, How much "too much" is too much? And how much "too much" is just right? We can all think of occasions when a joke has been milked to death, or a sketch outstays its welcome. Excess is a relative and evaluative concept. Part of the craft of comedy is knowing what and when and how to repeat, when and how to vary, how far to push something, when to hold back. A sketch from the Australian show *The Micallef Program* (ABC, 1999, S2:E6) is a master class in this kind of judgment. The premise of "Spiffington Manse" is to present a scene in the manner of Jane Austen, where the strait-laced characters keep knocking things over. Again, and again, and again. On paper, this

Figure 2.6. When is a wig too big? Mr. Pogg (Francis Greenslade), master of Spiffington Manse. *The Micallef Program* (ABC, 1998–2001, S2:E6).

sounds less than promising. Yet the masterly pacing and the balancing of variation against repetition make the sketch a model of comic construction. It also attains the remarkable quality—remarkable, since it would seem to be a contradiction in terms—of being excessive and restrained at the same time.

The basis for this lies in its parody of British period drama, sending up both the extravagance of the genre and the abstemiousness of its characters. This is a genre in which restraint is excessive and passion burns more brightly for being contained, hence the proverbial heaving bosoms. The *constant* talk of marriage prospects, the *sumptuous* costumes, the *obsession* with status and propriety are some of the sketch's parodic targets. Too-much-ness is everywhere in this sketch: hats too big, hems too wide, speech too verbose, gestures too mannered, the room too cluttered. But not . . . excessively so. The furnished interior of Spiffington Manse could plausibly indicate an upper-middle-class family with aristocratic pretensions that has outgrown its drawing room, and the costumes are (if not wholly accurate for the period) acceptably authentic for the genre, even the oversize bicorn hat worn by Shaun Micallef. One could imagine, in another sketch, this hat being gargantuan, twice the size, a more blatant visual gag about status. However, this would have overwhelmed other elements in the scene and given it a too singular prominence. Similarly, *most* of the lines and gestures one could imagine featuring in a straight period drama, even the occasional outburst of clumsiness, perhaps used to indicate the social awkwardness of a character. The over-the-top element here, of course, is the scale of disturbance and the fact that nobody seems to notice.

Unlike most sketches that announce their conceit within seconds, however, "Spiffington Manse" keeps its powder dry and builds the scene gradually. The parody is initially subtle, and the tone, sedate. After a title card and establishing shots of a manor house, accompanied by a string quartet playing chamber music, we find Flora (Roz Hammond), adorned in a classical gown with ribbons and frills, pacing in anticipation (we learn) of a marriage proposal, her hair ringlets bouncing with every excited movement. Mr. Pogg (Francis Greenslade), her father, in a leather armchair, wearing pince-nez spectacles and an outsized powdered wig, tells her to sit down and calm herself. When he confirms that he shares her hope of a proposal, she sits at his feet and recalls the chivalry of her suitor, specifically how he "saved Daisy from the bog." If the mental image of this, combined with the vulgar second meaning of "bog" (as lavatory, in Australian slang), encourages a modest titter, it's because it rebels against the emphasis on decorum in the dialogue, with its references to ladylike composure and gentlemanly valor. But this *double entendre* is really a red herring, or a mere item of punctuation, because the more important comic preparation is Mr. Pogg's attempt to subdue his daughter, keeping the lid on her puppylike behavior lest something should get broken, and the way she moves around to her father's side, darting through the gap between the armchair and a small table on which sits a tea set, the narrowness of the gap emphasized by the way her crinoline dress is squeezed as she passes through it. For a first-time viewer of the sketch, the idea that she might upset the tea set would probably be more or less subliminal. But, moments later, when she gets up once more and walks to the far side of the drawing room, she returns through this gap, and her skirt more noticeably brushes, although still does not topple, a precariously poised milk jug. At this point, her father jumps up from his armchair, urging Flora not to get into a "tither." (The sketch takes pleasure in rolling out ridiculous and archaic English phrases.) We hear a metal clatter as Mr. Pogg follows in Flora's wake, which, although prominent as a sound effect, could easily be written off as a mistake on the part of the sketch or, more complexly, as a "comic detail" on the part of the period drama (ah, the bumbling father, unable to keep a lid on his daughter's passions).

However, these are but the first steps in a carefully proportioned escalation of disturbance. As Mr. Pogg pursues his daughter behind the harpsichord, we hear a distressed *miaow* as someone treads on the tail of

Figure 2.7. Getting into a "tither." Anne Phelan, Francis Greenslade, Roz Hammond. *The Micallef Program* (ABC, 1998–2001, S2:E6).

an unseen cat. Immediately, so as to form a percussive one-two, we cut to a woman flinging the door open and hear a thud-crash as it knocks a swivel chair and topples a couple of empty sherry glasses that were resting on the nearby bureau. But the issue goes unremarked as Madame Pogg (Anne Phelan) sails into the room to express some concern about Flora. Mr. Pogg gruffly tells his wife, as he earlier told his daughter, to calm herself and, with that, the spate of minor upsets might appear to be over. The rhythm of the sketch might be broadly characterized as a series of bursts, each more vigorous than the last, followed each time by a brief spell of relative calm, typically punctuated by an incongruous and frankly inexplicable utterance. On this occasion, when Father asks Madame Pogg to fetch a brandy from the sideboard, she looks confused. "*Cyborg*?" she asks, quizzically. This is a different kind of disturbance, the surface of the sketch being momentarily ruptured by a single word from period drama's generic antithesis, science fiction. Impossible as it is that someone in the eighteenth century could mishear the everyday word "sideboard" for the yet-to-be-coined term "cyborg," this repeats later in the sketch, when Madame Pogg asks the servant to set some flowers in a vase on the sideboard. "The *cyborg*, Madame?" the servant asks. Again, nothing more is made of it—no succession of sci-fi references, no human-robot hybrid finally emerging from a cupboard. The anachronistic misconstruction just hangs there, out of place, and is then brushed away. It is made weirder by the fact that it is repeated once and no more. If it had become a series, the pattern would have made it a kind of refrain. A lesson in comedy: if gratuitousness is what you're after, two is the magic number.

 The first cluster of proper accidents is initiated when Madame Pogg leads Flora in the direction of a recuperative couch. As she reaches across the harpsichord to lead Flora by the arm, she knocks over a picture frame that was decoratively standing on the soundboard lid. Flora, in her hoop dress, then appears momentarily to become jammed between the harpsichord and a bird cage, before the maid (Sarah Adams) bursts through a side door (another *clang*) to announce the arrival of a suitor. In her excitement at this news, Madame Pogg spins around to tell the maid to fetch Daisy, and her trailing arm topples over a loaded cake stand, the clatter almost drowning out her instruction. To which the maid performs a curtsy, but before she exits, her sleeve catches on the crown of a decorative pineapple, causing a fruit bowl to crash to the floor. At which point, Captain Billing-Smythe (Shaun Micallef) promptly enters from the opposite door, his appearance marked by another clatter of unspecified objects and the felling of a wooden coat stand. By this point, the floor is littered with fallen items on which Captain Billing-Smythe stumbles to greet Madame Pogg. As he does so, his bicorne hat is knocked off by a low-hanging chandelier.

What keeps this repetitive business just the right side of repetitious, and wonderfully funny, is the degree of variation and the way each accident is inventively borne out of character. Madame Pogg's reaching over the harpsichord and knocking down the picture frame is the result of a credible concern to escort Flora, combined with the fact that soundboard lids of harpsichords are liable to be decorated with pictures. It is the extravagance of her sleeves, and of her gestures, that sends the cake stand flying. The fruit bowl is upset by the maid, and not restored, one feels, with a justified contempt for the masters, who will insist on displaying such pretentious and cumbersome food items as pineapples. Captain Billing-Smythe's clumsy entrance is a function of characteristic bluster and an unfamiliarity with domestic settings for a man more at home on the open sea. In this way, gratuitousness is balanced with just a nod toward psychological justification. There is also a pleasing variation in the foregrounding of deliberateness. Anne Phelan's action of turning to face the maid and theatrically raising her hand to issue her instruction is precisely executed so that her sleeve catches the cake stand midroute. In other words, it's recognizable as a strict piece of choreography. When Shaun Micallef gets his hat knocked off by the chandelier, on the other hand, it feels semi-improvised, not exactly an accident within the sketch (since of course the hat was designed to be tall and the chandelier placed to hang low), but with an openness to the contingent. One feels the hat could have fallen anywhere, but it happens to tumble straight into his hands for a fortunate catch. Similarly, when Daisy (Robyn Butler) enters holding the lead of a gigantic dog, it pulls her away from her mark, where she is supposed to receive flowers (to the audible amusement of Shaun Micallef, who almost flubs his line before rescuing himself from the giggles).

This all reaches a head when Captain Billing-Smythe leads Daisy in a country dance, accompanied by Flora on the harpsichord. Holding hands, they perform a brisk sideways movement toward an ivory figurine on a pedestal, somehow thus far unscathed, now sent crashing to the floor. At the same time, Billing-Smythe's sword sheath protrudes from his belt, and as he passes a round table it sweeps some random china items from its surface. Then, as if to finish the job, Billing-Smythe bows to his partner, and this flourish sends over the table, along with its remaining crockery. Their gamboling is shown in a long shot that takes in the whole room, including the maid struggling with an oversize bunch of flowers, Madame Pogg patting the hound, and Flora at the harpsichord. The busyness of the mise-en-scène thus magnifies the clutter of the room and the force of their charge as they clear a path through it. At the same time, the dance turns the drawing room into an arena and its furnishings into props in waiting. It calls for a mode of apprehension that *notices* that the space has been elaborately set up, action elaborately plotted, such that every corner of the room will eventually be brought into play, every decorative item finds its moment to be duly sent southward. So it is that chaos goes hand in hand with choreography, economy with excess.

Finally, it is essential to the effect that nobody is worried, in this world of tact and delicate sentiment, about the catastrophic mess being made of the drawing room. Nor is this spectacle of destruction the work of one rogue klutz whose cloddishness is politely ignored. Everyone is at it, and nobody seems the least concerned by the sight of yet another accident. Voices are just diligently raised to be heard over the sounds of crashing and banging and the clatter of metal and porcelain underfoot. Perhaps most surprisingly, the contagion of carelessness extends to the servants as well as the masters. The waiting staff are just as accident-prone, and just as blasé about the disarray they will, presumably, at some point, need to clear up. This fact refuses the metonymic neatness that would give the sketch as a comment on the destructiveness of the upper classes or on the blundering tendencies of the British Empire. It's a more universal problem, a problem of fit. We carry on as if we were graceful, sophisticated creatures. But our rooms are too small, already choked with furniture, and our gestures woodenly extravagant.

# 3

# Thought Experiments

## "Argument Clinic"

Harry Brighouse has observed that "some sketches are . . . rather like thought experiments; they say 'Of course, this couldn't happen or isn't going to happen. But let's ask what would make sense if it *did* happen" (2006: 63). This certainly rings true for a certain kind of absurdist sketch that proceeds from a "what-if" conceit and plays out a line of action. The development is typically to proceed by turning the screw, making the idea more concrete, more detailed, and more specific, before adding further "what-ifs" to the initial premise. But Brighouse is not just observing something about a sketch format—he wants to imply a kinship between sketch comedy and philosophy. His example is "Argument Clinic' from *Monty Python's Flying Circus* (BBC, 1972, S3:E3).

The sketch begins quietly, with Michael Palin meekly walking up to a receptionist and saying that he'd like to have an argument. She sends him down a corridor, where Mr. Barnard, in room 12, would be happy to oblige with a five-minute argument. The Client enters the first door and finds himself barked at by a belligerent man behind a desk (Graham Chapman) who calls him a "vacuous, toffee-nosed, malodorous pervert." There's been a mistake: this is Abuse. The Client needs the room next door. Palin knocks, enters, and asks the next suited man behind a desk (John Cleese) if this is the right room for an argument. "I've told you once," says Mr. Barnard, and—once the penny drops for the Client that the argument is *already* underway—the two fellows take turns disagree-

Figure 3.1. Michael Palin and John Cleese. *Monty Python's Flying Circus* (BBC, 1969–74, S3:E3).

ing with one another. Trouble is, they seem to disagree about what an argument *is*. Every time Palin's Client says, "You did not," Barnard has a tendency to say, "Yes, I did." "This isn't an argument," complains the Client. "It's just contradiction." "No, it isn't," replies Barnard.

What is an argument, anyway? "It's not just contradiction," says the Client, and he ventures a definition: "An argument is a collective series of statements to establish a definite proposition."

"No, it isn't."

The Client insists. "Argument is an intellectual process; contradiction is just the automatic gainsaying of anything the other person says."

"No, it isn't."

They haven't got any further before Barnard rings a bell, calling time on the argument and adopting a resting position. "That was never five minutes just now," says the Client. "I'm afraid it was," says Barnard. The Client sits forward excitedly: "No, it wasn't." Barnard won't take the bait. "Sorry, I'm afraid I'm not allowed to argue anymore," he says, and he tells the Client that if he wants to go on arguing, he'll have to pay for another five minutes. After some protest, the Client hands over a bill, which Barnard gratefully receives, and promptly denies that he has been paid. They dispute this for a moment, before the Client spots an advantage: "A-ha! Well if I didn't pay, why are you arguing?" "I could be arguing in my spare time," replies Barnard. At which point, the Client storms out of the room and off to the Complaints Department. "I want to complain," he declares, to the man in the next office (Eric Idle), who waits with his feet up on the desk. "*You* want to complain?" replies the man. "Look at these shoes, I've only 'ad 'em three weeks."

It really is a model of sketch construction, with its route along a series of doors, exemplary in its twists and turns. When the Client walks into the first room, for instance, he looks stunned by the outburst from the man behind the desk, whom he takes to be genuinely angry. We think we know better: Chapman is starting an argument. But he's not; he's delivering abuse. "Sorry." And so the premise expands: what if there were many varieties of hostility available to clients? We realize that behind each door along this corridor, an employee spends all day behind a desk, just waiting to become abusive, or argumentative, or . . . ? There is a *fizz* of possibility. And just as we adjust ourselves to entertain this revised premise, another part of the idea is turned on its head. We stay in the Abuser's office for a moment after the Client has departed, and watch Chapman's face turn into a snarl: "Stupid git." So the Abuser was *genuinely* annoyed by the disturbance! And the apology was the real performance: the tirade of practiced abuse was merely channeling his authentic anger, which he then had to suck down and suppress for the sake of professional courtesy.

Don't we know what an argument sounds like? Well, no, not exactly, since the sketch puts the concept in doubt. Palin's Client argues that an argument is not contradiction, ironically, by means of contradiction. "It isn't just saying 'No, it isn't,'" he insists. "Yes, it is," says Barnard. "No, it isn't," snaps the Client, and gives a puzzled look, as if briefly hearing some internal argumentative voice ("Yes, it is"). This is where Brighouse, in his eagerness to see the sketch as a demonstration of the merits of philosophical argument, seriously underestimates it. Brighouse sees an argument, as the Client defines it, as "an intellectual process" and wants to see the argument clinic as essentially a privatized, walk-in philosophy department, where those of us able to pay for the service may encounter "smart, good-willed and intellectually serious people to alert us to perspectives and reasons we would not have been able to conjure up on our own" (63). One suspects, here, that the academic Brighouse is rather too keen to see the sketch as valorizing his own sphere of business, perhaps sensing the benefits of a rebranding exercise. But it is a stretch too far to conclude, as Brighouse does, that it is, despite the apparent absurdity, "entirely sensible to go to an argument clinic (as the client understands it)" (63). This begs the question, how does Brighouse understand the Client to understand the business of the argument clinic? Brighouse asserts that the Client wants to be shown "what is wrong with his own beliefs and reasons for those beliefs" (56), to which I am tempted to reply: "No, he doesn't."

That is to say, there is precious little to support this view of Palin's Client. For one thing, the client makes zero effort to specify a topic he'd like to have an argument about, either when he speaks to the receptionist or when he meets his interlocutor. It's true, the poor sap hardly has time to introduce any controversial opinions of his own upon arrival in Mr. Barnard's office, where he is dropped into the middle of a dispute ("I've told you once . . ."). Even when the penny has dropped, however, and the client realizes the argument session is already underway, he does not attempt to steer the subject or pose a conundrum. Moreover, while he takes his seat with enthusiasm (a little bounce in his chair, clasped hands), this seems more like the excitement of someone poised for an almighty spat than someone ready to receive pearls of wisdom. He's spoiling for a verbal fight.

Brighouse's idea of an argument would certainly chime with that offered by the Client, as "a collective series of statements to establish a definite proposition"—a laughably ready-to-hand definition, as if the Client has swallowed a dictionary. That is *one* sense of the word, but it's far from the whole story, and Brighouse is naïve if he believes that's what Palin's Client really wants. Another definition of "argument," of course, is a heated, angry exchange. The *sparring* dimension of an argument, the sense of the word that suggests a live personal dispute, is notably missing from the Client's insipidly scholastic definition. Surely, if the Client had wanted a set of propositional statements, he could have gone to the library. Brighouse's main evidence for thinking the Client wants to hear an enlightened philosophical thesis seems to boil down to the customer's complaint that he "came here for a good argument," the adjective of which Brighouse takes to mean something like "substantive." But a "good argument" can also mean a bloody good row. A "good argument," in *that* sense, is a passionate, not a clinical, affair.

That's why the Client finds the whole business so disappointing. There's no pleasure to be taken in disputing someone, like Barnard, who has no real convictions, who is paid to disagree. In fact, although it may be a "clinic," there's no indication of any therapeutic purpose. Palin's Client tells the receptionist that he'd "like" an argument, not that he's been referred. When he tells her it's his first time, his hands hang boyishly down by his sides, and his fingers fiddle with the hem of his jacket. This place seems more like a bordello than a health center. That would make sense of its pay-per-five-minute policy. Perhaps, like a brothel, it's the last resort for those in need of passionate contact and unable to find it elsewhere. Maybe the lukewarm, conformist world outside has become so devoid of enmity, so jolly polite and accommodating, that the very prospect of disagreement has the thrill of taboo. That's presumably the rationale for casting Palin in the role of the Client: he seems such a *nice* man, hardly someone you'd expect to see here. It's always the quiet ones, as they say.

By contrast, there is no hint of the illicit in the behavior of Rita Davies's receptionist. The politeness of her demeanor is emphasized, in fact. If she has contempt or pity for the parade of weirdos who arrive at her desk each day, she certainly hides it well. We are given no reason to suspect any divergence between public manner and private attitude. However, we might retrospectively suspect her clerical breeziness is but the first in a series of behavioral fronts. There is Chapman's clinic practitioner, whom we gather keeps his genuine anger concealed, first behind a tirade of professionalized abuse, then behind the most sincere-seeming of apologies. Glimpsing this man behind closed doors, calling the intruder a "stupid git," might lead us to believe we are seeing his true character, a being closer to the seething maniac we first encountered than to the friendly persona he subsequently adopted, as it turns out in masquerade. But can we say for sure? He *could* be permanently crabby and ill-tempered, except when he makes an effort to conceal it, or he could be simply getting back into role in preparation for an expected next client.

This is partly a joke about characters in sketches. They are, in general, only what they show themselves to be, any one of them a type governed by a single characteristic that determines everything he does. Characters in sketches *are* their behavior. We are not invited to entertain a complex backstory or contemplate a range of possible motivations for their actions. But precisely because we can only go on the evidence of what we see and hear, we can't be confident in placing this Chapman character, either as a thoroughgoing curmudgeon who occasionally affects politeness, or as an affable type, at heart, who does a convincing turn as a raging lunatic.

Then there is Cleese as Mr. Barnard, who seems scrupulous and efficient but is in fact lazy and corrupt—or is this, too, part of the wider act, designed to provoke the longed-for wrath? When Barnard insists that the client's five minutes are up and that he is obliged to pay a further fee for an additional five minutes, do we take this as a cessation or a continuation of the argument? Is Barnard an incompetent arguer and furthermore a swindler or an expert arguer who knows precisely how to fuel a dispute? Either way, he's a slippery fish who may or may not be arguing in his spare time.

This is the sketch's other thought experiment: suppose a world where all dispositions are potentially simulated, to the extent that you are unable to tell where you stand with *anyone*. On reflection, this is not so very far from our own world. After all, since politeness is a matter of professional courtesy, how can you tell whether that deferential waiter likes or loathes you? Come to think of it, how can you can ever say, with confidence, who someone is, what they are doing, and why they are doing it? The very idea entices us to the brink of a skeptical abyss.

The sketch dangles that paranoid suggestion as it finally embarks on a journey to the land of infinite regression. From an argument about arguments, we nosedive into a spiral of self-reference. Following his encounter with the Complaints Department, Palin's Client promptly storms out and into the next room, where Terry Jones waits behind the door with a wooden mallet to bash him over the head. "No, no, no," says Jones, when Palin yells out. "Hold your head like *this* and then go 'Waaah.'" Apparently, it's "being-hit-on-the-head lessons" in this room. "What a stupid concept!" says Palin. By this point, the sketch is staging its own descent into the writing-room paper basket, having discovered a format (one room after another) where once-rejected sketch ideas can be given a brief, glorious showing. The obvious joke here is the self-deprecating notion that the Pythons are an undisciplined bunch who are unable to end their sketches (hence the famous refrain that self-consciously interrupts a sketch before the lack of a punchline becomes evident: "And now for something completely different"). However, this metareflection on the sketch troupe's inability to close out their material produces, ironically, a deeply satisfying ending.

Figure 3.2. Curtain call: Michael Palin, Eric Idle, John Cleese, Graham Chapman, and Terry Jones. The hand about to emerge from the doorway may or may not belong to Terry Gilliam. *Monty Python's Flying Circus* (BBC, 1969–74, S3:E3).

For all the appearance of radical self-sabotage, under the guise of disintegration, the ending grants something quite traditional: a good old-fashioned curtain call. There are music-hall conventions of direct address and even a chorus refrain. A police inspector (Graham Chapman, now dressed for his second role in the sketch in a detective-style overcoat) arrives on the scene, introduces himself as Inspector Fox of the Light Entertainment Police, Comedy Division, Special Flying Squad, and proceeds to make an arrest under section 21 of the Strange Sketch Act. He is interrupted by a second police inspector (Eric Idle, who has also now thrown on an overcoat), who introduces himself as Inspector Thomsons-Gazelle of the Program Planning Police and promptly announces his intention to charge everyone involved, citing offences against the Getting-Out-of-Sketches-without-Using-a-Proper-Punchline Act, which prohibits ending a sketch lazily by "just having a policeman come in." But the second inspector tails off, realizing he too, in his effort to close out the sketch, is falling foul of this act. Then the shoulder of the second inspector is clasped by the leather-gloved hand of a third inspector (John Cleese). And he, in turn, is, of course, clasped on the shoulder by the leather-gloved hand of a *fourth* inspector. But rather than seeing the queue of arresting inspectors stretches off down the corridor, and away to infinity, we cut to a black screen with the title "The End."

This business at the end is self-consciously "tacked on" to the Argument Clinic sketch proper, a structural appendage. But the Pythons found classical balance stifling and alluring in equal measure. For the final "extraneous" section, with its community of players joined in a kind of stage bow, serves a purpose after all, to counteract that earlier vision of society as a network of inscrutable others, each in his own separate room. And this in turn suggests comedy as an answer to skeptical despair or at least something to keep it at bay. For when we laugh at a gag or dig a sketch, we are never alone. We find ourselves in touch with those who share something with us; call it a sense of humor.

## "Gerald the Gorilla"

Some of the most memorable and weird philosophical thought experiments can be found in the work of Ludwig Wittgenstein. Cato Wittusen lists just some of the scenarios the philosopher asks us to consider:

> We are, for example, invited to imagine people apparently trading wood but where the setting of price was incomprehensible to us, a country that existed only for two minutes that was a projection of a part of England, a cave-man producing

Figure 3.3. I wanna be like you: Mel Smith and Rowan Atkinson. *Not the Nine O'Clock News* (BBC, 1979–82, S2:E5).

regular marks for himself, communication systems of builders, a child with deviant responses trying to follow a rule, people unacquainted with games sitting at a table performing the moves of a chess game, a speaking lion, and so on." (2010: 115)

One could imagine any one of these hypotheticals featuring as the basis of an absurdist sketch. The speaking lion is perhaps Wittgenstein's most famous thought experiment: "If a lion could talk, we could not understand him" (1953: 190). Perhaps this could be performed as a three-hander, with a pitiable translator trying to decipher the lion's politely articulated growls and roars and convey them in a form that satisfies the demands of a safari tourist who simply wants to know if there are any decent restaurants this side of the savannah. Even if that might not have legs as a full sketch, the very effort to envisage how it might be actualized helps to tease out one of Wittgenstein's implications, that understanding one another is dependent on leading broadly commensurate lives. How could a lion grasp the concept of a "restaurant," for example, let alone evaluate the merits of different restaurants, without having dwelled in the human life world—that is, eating in the sorts of places his questioner eats in rather than the "restaurants" he is used to patronizing on the savannah?

Conversely, even if we could imagine a lion "having" concepts and these being attached to lionish sounds or feline gestures in a patterned way, how could we grasp these concepts without having ourselves lived the life of a lion—for which *being* a lion is surely prerequisite?

We might also reflect on why, with all the animal kingdom to choose from, Wittgenstein chose a lion for the remark. One reason might be because, while not the most outlandishly alien of beasts, given our having crowned him "king" and our admiring his fluffy mane and penetrating gaze, a lion is perhaps the most iconically wild of creatures, the one most likely to turn unruly. Whereas what we normally mean by "talk" is a kind of civilized exchange. What would it mean for a lion, in the hypothetical sketch above, to growl *politely*? Or, for that matter, what do we presume that lion is saying to us every time he roars at the start of an MGM picture? This takes us closer to the paradox of Wittgenstein's aphorism, or, more accurately, its jokelike quality. It asks you to accept a premise in order that you refuse its possibility. For instance, the idea of speech (as distinct from random noises) supposes comprehensibility, yet Wittgenstein tells us that a lion's talk would be incomprehensible. Therefore, if a lion could talk, it could not really *talk*—not do the thing we do when we produce what we conveniently call "talk." Perhaps, to put it another way, if a lion could talk, it would no longer be a lion. In the standard account of human evolution, the acquisition of language was bound up with the acquisition of consciousness. In that case, we would have to imagine the advance from lion to talking lion as akin to the leap across the gulf that came to separate apes from hominids (a gulf that recent versions of *The Planet of the Apes* love to leap across).

But what if there were no significant existential divide between humans and beasts? What if our life world could truly be shared? This might be a delightful thought, speaking to our deep feeling of attachment to, and affection for, certain beasts and our fond wish that they could talk to us, as in *Dr. Doolittle* (1967). It is also the thought experiment of a well-loved sketch from *Not the Nine O'Clock News* (BBC, 1979–1982, S2:E5). "Gerald the Gorilla" takes the form of a mock TV interview with a bumptious academic (played by Mel Smith) who has been undertaking fieldwork in the area of animal communication. He is joined on the show by one of his experimental subjects, Gerald (Rowan Atkinson, in a full-body ape suit). The interviewer (Pamela Stephenson) asks the Wittgensteinian question: "Professor, can Gerald really 'speak,' as we would understand it?" The Professor reports that, yes, Gerald really can speak a few actual words, and he begins telling the story of Gerald's journey to this stage, starting with his King Kong–style capture from the Congo in 1967. Gerald the Gorilla corrects him: "'68." So not only can this gorilla utter a few actual words, but he understands the concept of time, grasps the Gregorian calendar, knows Arabic numerals, appreciates the modern convention of abbreviating years, has an excellent capacity for recall, and is, what's more, an obnoxious pedant. It turns out that Gerald has been staying in the Professor's house since the time of his capture and has evidently become socialized in the Professor's image. While this gorilla is infinitely more comprehensible than the aphoristic lion, the implication of the gag shares with Wittgenstein's remark the idea that the business of "talking" far exceeds the mere forming of sounds to manifest words and sentences to match thoughts, drive actions, describe perceptions, and so on. To be able to "talk" is to inhabit a lifeworld of beliefs, values, and conventions, all of which are invoked, if not necessarily endorsed, in the use of a language.

The remarkable extent of Gerald's socialization is amusingly conveyed before he even speaks. As Wittgenstein reminds us, gesture is also part of human language, and even the first mute images of Gerald, sitting patiently in the chair beside his keeper, show him to be articulate in this respect. Rowan Atkinson's performance has Gerald loosely mirroring the Professor's comportment, his hairy legs urbanely crossed in a state of rest, and when the host announces Gerald's name, the gorilla gives a brief nod in the direction of the studio audience. This nod-to-audience gesture is deeply familiar to anyone who has watched public interviews, but the convention is made curious again by the use of the ape costume. It's a kind of confirmation of identity in response to the giving of a name ("correct") combined with the receipt of a greeting ("I accept your welcome"), the communication of readiness to proceed, *and* the acknowledgment of an essentially friendly audience. For this gesture to be performed correctly, the shoulders should stay pretty much still while the head nods, ideally with a slight bounce: a sharp nod with no bounce would be too curt; a turn of the shoulders would turn the nod more into a stage bow. What a strange and intricate language we speak, even when we use no words!

The Professor, meanwhile, with an equally familiar gesture, briefly brushes his clothed knee with his hand, as if to rid it the suit of some specks of gathered dust, although this seems more an unconscious gesture betraying self-regard in the preparation for public display. This little move is echoed moments later when Gerald examines his own nails. The way he stretches out his fingers makes the gesture conceited, slightly feminine (a bit like checking the intactness of nail gloss), and above all calculated to make himself conspicuous while the Professor is talking up his own scientific achievements. Gerald's finger-check gesture emphasizes the extent to which the gorilla has overcome his natural dispositions and become so comprehensively socialized. Indeed, both the knee brush and the finger check are the gestures of an advanced society, imbued with cultural meanings around respectability, patience, and self-esteem. But they are also instances of self-grooming and expressions of dominance, a distant echo of the way primates police their fur for ticks and fleas and signal their status through display.

We see this alpha-male rivalry more blatantly when the interview degenerates into territorial squabbling. As the Professor begins to tell the host about his work, Gerald interrupts: "If I might just *butt in* at this point, too, I think I should point out that I have done a considerable amount of work on this project *myself*." This is a very English circumlocution, a way of softening an interjection in order to make it more socially acceptable ("If I might just . . . ," "I think I should . . ."), but it essentially amounts to "Fuck you, you moron" or perhaps an aggressive growl. The Professor, visibly riled, puts Gerald back in his place with a similarly circuitous preamble: "I'm sorry, I'm sorry, can I put this into some sort of perspective? When I *caught* Gerald—'(pause and a meaningful look, to make the word sting)'—in '68, he was completely wild." "Wild?" replies Gerald. "I was absolutely *livid*."

"Absolutely *livid*" is without question the knockout line of the sketch and brilliantly conceived. For one thing, there is no strain in the way this double meaning is set up, because it follows smoothly from the idea that the Professor is wishing to insist on Gerald's animal nature and seems entirely credible that Gerald, as a nonnative speaker, should mistake what the Professor means by "wild" (which can mean both "uncivilized" and "cross"). The line is, in fact, a double double meaning because "completely," as the Professor means to use it, is a synonym for "fully," but it can also mean "very." So the misconstruction (i.e., that the Professor was saying that Gerald was very cross when he was captured) is actually a consequence of Gerald's remarkable command of the English language rather than his lack of fluency. In fact, it suggests an extraordinary absorption in his adopted culture, to the extent that the very particular English middle-class meaning of "wild" (to mean something like "outraged") is more native to him than the memory of untrapped and untamed animal freedom. The word "livid" is also brilliantly chosen, being the most euphemistic and genteel of synonyms for "angry." Whereas "absolutely furious" might well have summoned the image of a raging gorilla, "absolutely livid" is the kind of expression used by little old ladies to convey their displeasure at a social snub. Rowan Atkinson's delivery of the line is also expertly judged. He doesn't land on the word "livid" like a punchline, which might have conveyed a sense of being too pleased with his own cleverness, but carries on in character, muttering inaudibly. This is not just a neat way of keeping the diegetic situation going during a period of extended studio laughter. It also develops the notion that the ostensibly traumatic event of his capture is now little more than a topic of grumbling resentment. There is also the matter of Rowan Atkinson's voice, which is both nasal and clipped, punctilious in the way he slightly lingers on each hard consonant (those who know his work on *Blackadder* [BBC, 1983–1989] will recall his pronunciation of "Baldrick"). That makes "livid" the perfect word for Atkinson to suggest the gorilla's slightly fey fastidiousness. The idea that Gerald has become obsessive about hygiene is confirmed later when he discloses that he spends most of his pocket money on carpet cleaner.

That anal quality of Gerald manifests as overcompensation for the embarrassing persistence of instinct. When he is not found scrubbing his own shit stains off the floor, this gorilla is inclined to eat a banana with a fork. He may not be able to resist having a snack midinterview, but his manners are *impeccable*. He takes similar pride in his appreciation of music. When the Professor complains about Gerald playing Johnny Mathis's *When a Child Is Born* at full volume during unsociable hours, the gorilla defends himself by observing that "the production on that album is amazing." The choice of that particular song for the gag is presumably to indicate that Gerald has failed to cultivate a taste beyond schmaltz. Yet he has mastered the metropolitan discourse of connoisseurship (the reference to the album's "production") as an alibi for obsessive, antisocial behavior.

If the exchange about Johnny Mathis makes Gerald the precocious (1950s) teenager, it makes the Professor a parent who has come to begrudge his child, undecided as to whether he resents Gerald's dependence or his independence. At other times, it's more a professional rivalry between these two, such as when the smart aleck Gerald leaps to correct the Professor's misuse of a technical term ("It's a whoop, a *whoop* of gorillas—it's a flange of baboons"). Elsewhere, they seem like an old married couple, especially when the conversation turns to the topic of Gerald's mother (who has apparently never liked the Professor, much to his hurt and annoyance). It's the Professor who comes off worse: Mel Smith renders him an ill-tempered sourpuss with a chip on his shoulder. This all begs the question: What would we become, if another species learned our ways? Apes are often said to be our "cousins": members of an extended family with whom we engage occasionally, happily enough, though without intimacy. How would this change if they moved in with us, learned our language, "aped" our ways? Would we find it charming, curious, companionate—or frustrating, sinister, maddening? The ambivalence is registered in the faintly repellent quality of Atkinson's ape mask, with its static, open mouth and the way it makes it seem he is perpetually rolling his eyes. Why is it disturbing? Perhaps it reminds us of our own grotesque unnaturalness, the cost of being able to talk.

## "Toilet Party"

What if things were different? Comedy, philosophy, and politics are bedfellows in begging this question. The radical provocations of Luis Buñuel's 1974 feature *The Phantom of Liberty* have often been linked with its rejection of conventional forms of narrative (e.g., Suleiman [1978]; Humphries [1995]; Tobias [1998]). As Michael Wood (2000) describes it, "The structuring principle of *The Phantom of Liberty* is a kind of chain: we start inside a story and leave it to follow one of its minor characters, who now becomes the major character in the next story" (32). However, emphasizing the way it departs from the standard narrative procedures of feature-length movies might lead us to neglect its closer screen relative, the sketch show. The humor of *The Phantom of Liberty* is simultaneously broad and dry and might be said to court amused perplexity more than outright laughter—but humor it is, and if we take the film's tip to relinquish our concern with narrative causality, the film's dozen or so

Figure 3.4. The guests take their seats. From left to right: François Maistre, Maryvonne Ricaud, Alix Mahieux, Marie-France Pisier, Jean Rougerie. *The Phantom of Liberty* (Luis Buñuel, 1974).

stand-alone scenes come to seem less like a perpetually digressive narrative and more like a succession of absurdist sketches.

Undoubtedly, the most renowned of its sequences is a depiction of a social function where, instead of sitting on chairs around a dinner table to share a meal, the hosts and their guests sit around a table that is strewn with nothing more than a few magazines and an ashtray, each person parked on an individual toilet, urinating and defecating as they chat. This episode is linked to a previous sketch, in which a professor (François Maistre) has been invited to give an anthropology lecture, of all things, to a group of gendarmes in a police training academy. The Professor has been lecturing the officers on the relativity of customs and the prospect of an evolution in society that might lead to a change in morals and behavior. He then warns about the potentially horrifying consequences of such an upheaval, and as an example "taken at random" he recounts a recent social visit to his friends' house. It's not exactly clear what lesson he expects the officers to take from the anecdote. The expectation that it will illustrate a horrifying upheaval of values is undermined by his behavior and dialogue in the scene, which confirms, quite rightly for the comic effect, that everything we see is entirely normal in this social universe. Nonetheless, the framing of the episode as a didactic device places it for us as something like a thought experiment.

We see the Professor and his wife (Jenny Astruc) arrive at their bourgeois friends' house, where they are welcomed by the host couple (Jean Rougerie and Alix Mahieux), their young daughter (Maryvonne Ricaud), and family friend Mme Calmette (Marie-France Pisier), engaging in the standard bourgeois pleasantries. The host comments on the guests' lateness, which is explained by bad traffic, and says that they almost started without them, a remark that may seem ill-tempered but that will shortly take on a more vivid meaning. In fact, everything seems normal until the hostess shows them to their places and assigns each shitter an individual throne according to the standard boy-girl seating arrangement. The emphasis on etiquette is important, of course, for the incongruous effect of the substitution, the gleaming rows of cream porcelain latrines, the formal symmetry of which the camera will shortly emphasize by adopting a frontal angle and settling down to a lower level with the guests as they assume their positions. The ensuing conversation establishes that the relation between eating and shitting, in terms of social acceptability, has not only been reversed, but proportionately reversed. For example, the Professor asks to be excused for his forthrightness when he reports that his recent trip to Spain was ruined because Madrid smelled so strongly of *food*. "Really indecent," he comments. That the strength of the food/eating taboo is exactly equivalent to our society's shit/shitting taboo is confirmed when the host family's daughter announces that she's hungry and her mother scolds her for saying such things at the table.

Maintaining all other recognizable norms is also important for the nature of a thought experiment: imagining a *single* norm changed in an otherwise recognizable social universe allows us to speculate about what other consequences might ensue. For instance, no sooner have the guests hitched their skirts and dropped their trousers than the conversation turns to high culture: Charles, the host, lowering his bared buttocks onto his seat, reports that he and his wife recently went to the opera and saw a successful production of *Tristan and Isolde*. Given the context, this prompts the thought that if the traditional hierarchy between the upper and lower body were reversed, turned upside-down, wouldn't other conventional hierarchies follow suit? How would French culture be organized differently if operatic flatulism were an art form of distinction, and gastronomy, a sordid practice? What would the history of taste look like if "taste" itself were a dirty word?

A similar question arises with regard to social opinions and politics. The hostess laments that at the opera the soprano performer, who otherwise gave a delightful performance, had gained weight. This suggests that large bodies might remain objects of scorn in this alternative society, though perhaps rebuked less for overeating than for underevacuating. Charles raises the topic of population growth (a familiar reactionary concern of the bourgeoisie) and the issue of industrial waste despoiling rivers. The Professor adds that the projected increase in human bodily waste is also a concern, and the gathered company proceeds to debate how much shit and piss is produced by a single person in one day. This is perhaps the mirror of dinner-party concerns about agricultural overproduction, food mountains being a more acceptable dinner-table topic than heaps of excrement. By way of illustration, the Professor refers the party to the nearby fish tank, clouded with fish feces, and the camera pulls back to view the party through the tank's milky haze. It leads one to wonder if environmental pollution would be higher up our political agenda if waste production in personal terms weren't quite so hidden from view.

Besides the parallel, however, there is also a contrast between the cloudy fish tank and the dinner party itself, namely that, in the world of pet fish, consumption and defecation are not compartmentalized activities. Pet fish shit where they eat, and vice versa. For all their spatial unfreedom, pet fish have a kind of liberty in this regard that is not afforded by the human regime of assigning different aspects of bodily function to discrete spaces, policed by socially conditioned responses such as disgust and with the arrangement of course justified on health grounds. The alternative world of the toilet party, for all its oddness, maintains the location and strength of the boundary between public and private that we have in our own world; it's just that the sides have been flipped.

Is it *arbitrary* that we are content to eat together but prefer to defecate alone? After all, the distinction between public and private is socially prescribed, and communal latrines have been an important feature of societies in other times. It's difficult to imagine that we could ever prefer colonic perfume to the odor of food, but perhaps that just illustrates the strength of our conditioning. (How, for example, would Gerald the Gorilla regard all this or have regarded it before his socialization?) We are asked to entertain such thoughts when the Professor excuses himself from the toilet in order to pay a visit to the dining room. The discreet way he asks the maid directions, in a lowered voice, and the way he glances round at the table and straightens his jacket on departure are familiar gestures to us, but which here seem so ridiculous. It highlights the way we conspire, with verbs like "freshen up" and euphemisms like "bathroom," to disavow what we know to be true about where so-and-so is going and the activity they will shortly, in a room just down the hall, be conducting—as if it were something immoral and illicit.

That is exactly what is suggested by the tenor of the Professor's behavior as he enters the dining room, locks the door (for whose sake?), and takes a seat. He pulls down a wall-mounted table, the drop-down function of which is less about saving space, one gathers, than about the fact that it can be stowed away, a further compartment to keep the activity it supports out of mind (the equivalent of the toilet lid). Everything about the design of this room is deliberately uncomfortable; it is not somewhere to dwell. The lighting is harsh, and the seat, no more than practical. The drop-down table feels a bit unsteady, and its metal flip-down leg makes an unpleasant scraping sound when it is positioned on the hard floor. The food is summoned by pressing a button at the side of a hatch (as in an elevator). Evidently, it is someone's job, somewhere, to *prepare* this food (just as there is a whole industry of people who work at sewage plants), but the very thought of their labor is apparently best kept at bay. There is an excessive attempt to keep it all impersonal, strictly functional.

Whisper it, though: the Professor seems to take a certain *pleasure* in this activity behind the locked door. With the tray in place, he rubs his hands in anticipation. We hear a slimy sound effect (meat juice and/or saliva) as he lifts the greyish chicken leg to his open mouth and an almost gravellike crunch as he greedily tears off the end of a baguette. At that point, he is interrupted by someone trying the door, and with a mouth full of food—a sight unavailable, thank goodness, to the young woman outside—he barks that the room is occupied. What makes the

Figure 3.5. Nature calls. François Maistre. *The Phantom of Liberty* (Luis Buñuel, 1974).

scene funny and faintly nauseating is aided, above all, by the color scheme of that private dining room: grey and milky, recalling the fouled fish tank. But the commingling of food and shit, of eating and defecating, happens only in our imagination. Or rather, not "only." Imagination is, after all, the precinct polite society works hardest to police.

If sketch comedy is drawn to the "what-if" scenario, it is perhaps because, like the philosophical thought experiment, it licenses the imagination to range over things we habitually take for granted, to entertain or stake out ideas we might otherwise dismiss as preposterous. Unlike the thought experiment proper, however, comedy is not typically didactic. "Argument Clinic" does not venture a new definition of "argument" or offer a position piece on philosophical skepticism. "Gerald the Gorilla" does not place itself to reveal the true existential relation between humans and beasts or whether they could share a language. Buñuel's scene of evacuation and consumption does not prove that the relation between private and public is arbitrarily drawn. But they do put these ideas into play. In so doing, they generate a productive confusion on matters we took to be settled.

# 4

# Prime Numbers

## "Breakfast"

Sketch comedy's origins in variety theater give one explanation for why so many skits are musical in character. Notable musical sketches range from twisted chorus lines, like the lumberjack song in *Monty Python's Flying Circus* ("I cut down trees / I skip and jump / I go to the lavatory"), to choreographed mimes, such as the marital spat synchronized to Beethoven's Fifth (starting with its conjugal finger-wagging to "du-du-du-duuuuh") performed by Sid Caesar and Nanette Fabray for *Caesar's Hour* (Shellrick Productions, 1954), to music video spoofs like the boy band parody "Girl, You Don't Need Make Up" from *Inside Amy Schumer* (Jax Media, 2015) ("You'll be the hottest girl in the nation / With just a touch of foundation"). Beyond defined song-and-dance numbers, it might even make sense to speak of the inherent musicality of comedy. Many sketches that feel a long way from the music hall can be found to be structured like popular songs (and roughly the same duration). Take, for example, the alternation of something like verse and chorus in two twenty-first-century examples discussed earlier, in Mitchell and Webb's "Sir Digby Chicken-Caesar" sketch, where each segment ends with a reprisal of *The Devil's Gallop*, and in Key and Peele's "Awkward Conversation," where the predictable sarcastic aside ("O-kaaay") offers a kind of refrain. The kinship runs deep.

The British double act of Eric Morecambe and Ernie Wise, best known for *The Morecambe and Wise Show* (BBC, 1968–77), highlighted the continuity between music hall and television comedy more than most. Each

Figure 4.1. Ernie Wise and Eric Morecambe. *The Morecambe and Wise Show* (BBC, 1968–77, S9:E6).

episode started with the duo—Ernie, sensible and squat; Eric, bespectacled, tall, and zany—doing a "spot" in front of some tan drapes that explicitly recalled variety theater. The show's assortment of bits and pieces always featured at least one musical interlude or finale, often with a celebrity guest, and typically disrupted by the antics of an unruly Eric. The show, invariably brought to a close with an amateur sing-song rendition of "Bring Me Sunshine," contained sketches based in domestic locales and everyday situations, often set in the duo's fictional "shared flat." Taking a leaf from Laurel and Hardy, and like Jim Henson's comic duo Bert and Ernie from *Sesame Street* (Children's Television Workshop, 1969–present), Eric and Ernie could often be found sharing a bed. At its best, Morecambe and Wise discovered new ways of combining cabaret with the everyday. The definitive example is "Breakfast" (S9:E6), in which the live-in couple synchronize their morning dining ritual to the plush sounds of David Rose and His Orchestra, fusing the two meanings of the word "routine."

We open with Eric and Ernie eating breakfast at the kitchen table. The domesticity of the space, in this opening shot, is marked by its lack of front. Our initial access is not via a proscenium presentation but through a diagonal view. This angle emphasizes the table corner (rather than its front edge) and compresses the space, making it feel boxed in. In the background, the kitchen radio is on, justifying the lack of conversation. Each man is in his own morning bubble, consuming his individual bowl of cereal. It is notable that these figures, who are regularly to be found fronting a show in matching suits or even tuxedos, here wear ordinary, unmatching dressing gowns, and they are turned inward, with no acknowledgment of the audience and no indication in their posture of being "on" or even of being with the other. We are about to witness, in terms of Michael Fried (1988), a movement from absorption to theatricality.

The radio's male presenter announces that the next song will be "The Stripper." As soon as we recognize the song's opening sassy bars, with its connotations of nightclub exhibitionism, we detect a change in the room. The start of some kind of coordination is felt in the cut to a closer view of Ernie when the tune begins, a cut so precise it has the quality of a mechanical switch. The song is timed to action in such a way that the opening trombone slide seems almost to summon Ernie to a standing position, and its swing beat continues the momentum, transporting him somnabulistically across the kitchen to seek out, as we discover, some bread. In order to take in Ernie's movement, the camera zooms out, giving a widening of perspective that matches the music as it broadens into a brass ensemble. Yet, despite the nod toward synchronization, Wise performs his journey with a natural waddle that resists turning it into a two-step (and spoiling the gradual line of development).

The wider view now allows us to take in the space of the bijou kitchen. The frontal view makes it a degree more theatrical, but it is cramped, hardly the place for a floor show. The small central breakfast table is surrounded by counters and cabinets on all four sides, providing barely enough width for a single person to walk comfortably past and around it. Ernie has headed towards us, to a kitchen counter that runs right along the front of the space, as in a cooking demonstration, adjoining an invisible "fourth wall" through which we now peer. On the surface of this counter, to the left, sits a bag of sliced bread and a glass bowl. At right angles to this counter, down the left-hand side of the kitchen, lies another preparation surface with grapefruits waiting their turn on a chopping board. In the left-back corner is the toaster, and, next to it, the refrigerator. All of these areas and items will eventually be brought into the routine.

For the meantime, however, there is nothing showmanlike about the way Ernie retrieves two slices of bread from the bag. It is Eric, now rising in the background, who gives the first theatrical turn. When he stands up, he takes an indirect route over to the toaster, getting up to the left and describing an arc all the way around the back of his chair. This is a rather impractical way of getting around the kitchen (it would have been quicker just to get up and head right, that is, straight to the device), and, as such, it feels decorative, like a dancer's turn, while also being heavy-footed, a perfunctory plod. Casual at it looks, it allows Eric to hit his mark precisely for the start of the routine proper. He arrives on the scene just in time to catch the bread that Ernie, on musical cue, has flung across the kitchen. In synchronization with a pair of percussive tripartite accents, the two bread slices are, one by one, thrown by one man, caught by the other, and tidily slotted into the toaster.

The coordination here is delightful precisely because it is imperfect. The neatness of the choreography is offset by the nonchalance with which it is performed. This is not the precision movement of trained dancers; nor is it the casual cool of the performer who declares his own brilliance by giving the impression he's not even trying. The whole business is carried out with a kind of indifference, as if it were just the normal way of preparing toast. Ernie continues to chew, for instance, as he chucks the bread across the room. Eric catches it with a deadpan expression, and with nothing so much as a flourish, and pops it into the toaster without ceremony.

The musical phrase to which the action is choreographed has a tripartite structure, in swing time, with the three stages of the action timed to coincide with three musical hits: a brass stab high for the bread toss ("BAH"); a slide whistle for the catch ("wheeee"); a percussive triangle to attend the plunge into the toaster ("ting"). This is more difficult than it sounds. In order to maintain coordination with the music, the plunging action needs to happen in the split-second interval after the slide whistle "wheeee" and in time with the triangle "ting." In that interval, the bread has to be caught, twisted to the right angle, and plunged, all in a single fluid action. Moreover, as anyone should know, it is tricky to put soft bread into a slot at speed. The slice is liable to bend, and, here, that would throw the action out of synch. Our recognition of this challenge generates a kind of aesthetic suspense. (For an elaboration of the concept of aesthetic suspense, see Clayton 2016.) Can they make it happen? Can they keep up with the music?

The first feat is achieved, and with the toaster stocked, Ernie gives a little "job done" nod, and each man turns away from the other, briefly presenting his back to the camera. If it weren't for the music, we could imagine they were about to regress into a mode of everyday separateness. However, this back turn is just a way of marking the end of act 1. When we cut into a side of view of Eric, ostensibly searching through cupboards for some ingredient or other, we notice that his formerly lethargic posture now has a bounce to it. The music offers a repeat "verse," but now in regular, rather than swing, time. Eric responds to this change by opening and shutting cupboard doors to the tempo. Both the cupboards are double, with twin doors opening both left and right.

His sideways movement along the row, going to each cupboard in turn and opening their doors sequentially, thereby provides the occasion for a rhythmic shimmy, a left-right shoulder action in time with the regular one, two of the beat. When, at the end of the row, he finds a bowl of eggs, Eric turns with a silly grin and sashays back along the line in a kind of cakewalk, arriving back near the toaster at the end of the verse. He marks the return with an ornamental back step and picks up an egg with a conjuror's flourish.

Meanwhile, Ernie has wandered back into the frame and resumed his position at the kitchen counter. The parallel left-to-right movement of both figures makes them feel linked by an invisible string. But, while Eric has notably perked up, Ernie's posture remains slumped. An injection of liveliness will now overtake him, too. In a mirror image of the earlier bread throwing, Eric abruptly tosses a succession of eggs across the room, and Ernie snaps into action, catching, cracking, and breaking them one by one into a bowl in a continuous stream of movement. This task proves even more challenging than Eric's toaster work. This time, Ernie is charged to accompany a *three*-part musical accent (octave high, octave low, with a silent beat interval between them) with a *four*-stage action (the throw, the catch, the crack, the break). If Eric found it tricky to catch bread and plunge in a fluid motion, it would be a Herculean feat for Ernie to crack and break eggs with the single continuous motion required by the tempo. (You actually need to crack the shell and then lift the egg before opening it into the bowl, so it is virtually a five-stage action: throw, catch, crack, lift, break.) The haste demanded by this near-impossible regime means that, by the time Ernie has deposited the third egg and turned to receive the fourth, the counter is spattered with albumen, and the bowl contains large fragments of eggshell. On receiving the final egg, Ernie "gives up" and hurls it unbroken into the mix. Yet the idea that the performer is conceding defeat is balanced by the way the yellow splash of this egg bomb actually matches the resolution of the musical phrase, sharply and perfectly, like an exclamation mark.

The on-cue egg splash exemplifies the way the sketch feels both messy and neat at the same time. This is a key part of the sketch's charm. One of the most delirious moments, later in the sketch, is the sight of Eric, armed with a cleaver and accompanying another musical crescendo, working his way along a row of grapefruits with maniacal chopping technique, raising the cleaver above his head each time and bringing it violently down through the fruit. The fact that the sliced halves are uneven, that Eric never quite manages to chop the grapefruit down the middle, is a delightful detail, far more pleasing, on this occasion, than if he had achieved a perfect run. Just as, at the circus, the clown's visible wobble as he mounts the balance ball makes his feat more exciting, there is a thrill that issues from the quality of "only-just-made-it." It gives, moreover, the assurance that these performers are not superhuman, not trained acrobats. Nor even Chaplins or Fred Astaires. The touch of inelegance bridges the gap between them and us, makes us feel that perhaps we could just about do that, like them. That it may be within our reach, too, to transform the everyday into a carnival.

Ernie's hurling of the egg into the bowl also marks the start of a new phase, where the sexual connotations of the music—this is, after all, stripper music—start to be brought into play. Ernie's yolky explosion, greeted by Eric with an ostentatiously aroused double take, is the first in a series of visual innuendos, or rather half-innuendos, since they do not call for leering acknowledgment in the manner of a *Carry On* (Sid James proffering a sausage roll to the face of Joan Sims) or Benny Hill (watering flowers with a hose held at crotch level). Yet, there is the sight of Ernie whisking those eggs. Without putting too fine a point on it, his energetic thrashing (watched attentively by Eric, who stands and stares in the background) is matched to a horn crescendo, culminating in a big-band vibrato and a triangle roll that echoes the convulsions of Ernie's hand movement. After each bout of beating, he looks positively spent. The vaguely sexual imagery returns, moments later, when Eric and Ernie each picks up a couple of grapefruit halves and gives them a vigorous twist and squeeze. Finally, there is the moment when Eric opens the

Figure 4.2. Eric Morecambe and Ernie Wise. *The Morecambe and Wise Show* (BBC, 1968–77, S9:E6).

fridge. The lighting changes drastically so that the white light from the fridge casts the only beam, and Ernie takes off his dressing gown in its cold/warm glow, like a striptease artist taken by the mood in something like orgasmic revelry. On which cue, Eric promptly pulls out an enormous line of sausages (in fact, one line for him and one line for Ernie). The two men promptly start gyrating and swirling their pendulous meat around the kitchen. They brandish these chains of sausages like whips and feather boas and dance with them to the end of the tune, exiting the kitchen—off, one can only surmise, to bed.

I take this wonderfully unholy synthesis of the domestic, the theatrical, and the erotic as a psychedelic vision of gay marriage before such a thing were dreamt of in television's public imaginary. If one feature of bourgeois marriage is the entanglement of the mundane and the sexual, in this sketch, the domestic and the erotic go hand in hand, the latter awoken out of the former by theatricalizing the private realm. The comic exhilaration of the sketch is its liberating answer to the age-old question: how does a relationship renew itself? It is the music issuing from the kitchen radio that initially seems to enliven the tired domestic scene. Yet the sketch ends, with a blow synchronized to the song's final note, with Eric sinking a cleaver into that radio, picking up the casing, and revealing it to be nothing but a prop, an empty shell, with no mechanism there at all. I take this otherwise puzzling final detail as a gesture of hope in our capacity to rejuvenate our relationships without external promptings, to say something like: we need no radio to enliven breakfast. That is, no escape is needed to counter domesticity's toll. It's up to each of us, each of us as a pair, to act on the resolve for renewal, to foster the mood for it, to turn every day into a dance. All that is needed is the willingness to coordinate, and the ability to see metaphorically.

## "Boardroom"

Even solo comedy can be a kind of double act. Music is a worthy partner. Five years after his split from Dean Martin, Jerry Lewis undertakes to do a skit by himself, with only the merest of props, and no dialogue, his motions matched to a big band number, "Blues in Hoss' Flat," played by Count Basie and His Orchestra. Near the end of *The Errand Boy* (Jerry Lewis, 1961), a sketch film set in a Hollywood studio, the eponymous dogsbody enters a boardroom to deliver some papers to the executive's desk. Finding himself alone, he takes a seat at the head of the boardroom table and playacts being the boss. Then he leaves.

There is nothing funny in the idea. The humor in this sketch is all about the execution. When, in 2010, the producers of the animated

Figure 4.3. Jerry Lewis. *The Errand Boy* (Jerry Lewis, 1961).

sitcom *Family Guy* secured Jerry Lewis's blessing to have the show's main character, Peter Griffin, play out the routine in full (Fox, S8 E9), the main homage paid by the "remake" (as these things often go) was to show up how much better the original was. For all the ostensible advantages of animation for "Mickey Mousing," its production process did not yield more precise synchronization because some of the timing is off. Beyond this, though superficially a gesture-by-gesture copy, the remake strikingly fails to live up to the earlier performance. The result is strangely banal.

About a decade ago, I tried to describe the Lewis sequence, although without the space (in a chapter about the relation between body and voice in slapstick) for more than a brief account. Here is my earlier description, more or less, in full:

> Taking a load off in the boss's leather armchair, he assumes the role by helping himself to a fat cigar and lighting it in his mouth. On the soundtrack, a plucked double bass tentatively begins a steady rhythm. Then, as he pulls out the cigar and gestures towards an imaginary board-member across the table, the first musical phrase, a brassy double-stab, issues from the soundtrack to fill his rubber-mouthing of a word of instruction to his associate. Pointing around the table to the rest of his invisible board members, he now enunciates more directives, mouthing seamlessly to fit the shape and rhythm of the song. The brass ensemble provides a sound

> that perfectly embodies the rasping voice of an egotist. His gestures are of the swaggering big man, almost cross-eyed in his arrogance, proclaiming his superior status with sweeping hand movements and an outsized puff on his cigar in the brief interval between melodic phrases. As the music builds up to fever pitch, he spins full circle on his leather chair and launches into an angry tirade, banging on the desk and waving his arms as the trumpets blare furiously to the motions of his mouth. (Clayton 2007: 143–44)

As far as it goes, as a summary description of the sketch, I would probably revise little of this. However, it now seems to me deficient as an account of humor. The *Family Guy* remake, produced after I wrote those words, could also be described in these terms (aside perhaps from the word "seamlessly"). So what are the aspects, unmentioned in the above account, that contribute to the superior achievement of the *Errand Boy* version? What is the difference that makes all the difference?

The answer is, of course, the fine detail. Lacking Jerry's facial mobility, the animated Peter Griffin cannot hope to emulate the fluid shifts and switches that mark Lewis's performance or realize its extraordinary compression of attitudes and imagery. Take, for example, the act of lighting of the cigar and pointing, in synch with that first "brassy double stab," at the first imaginary board member. In the *Family Guy* version, Griffin grabs a cigar from the box, lights up, and sits for a moment with it in his mouth (with eyelids low to indicate lazy self-gratification, perhaps) before pointing across the room with a sideways look (the dot pupils move to the right). There is no shift in persona as he goes through the routine, and his expression remains pretty much neutral throughout. By contrast, when Lewis takes the cigar from the box, he does so with a quick, furtive look around the room, with a chickenlike head movement that emphasizes his lowly status. Yet the character that snaps into existence with the first pointing gesture is supremely assured, right at home in the boss's chair. The gesture is like a smarmy game show host awarding a point to a contestant. It is accompanied by a brief flash of an approving smile to Jerry's imaginary opposite, as if he were noting an astute, or suitably ingratiating, remark from a junior executive. But then, not to cede too much to this young upstart, he pulls back to look at his cigar, crossing his legs in the brief interval between melodic phrases, a detail that suggests that he is merely patronizing this invisible man's presence in the boardroom. The merest lick of the lips (clearing a speck of tobacco debris) confirms the transformation of persona: the chicken has become a wolf.

Cocksure, authoritatively relaxed, certain of his status, this is all Mr. Big Man, with no residual hint of the anxious errand boy. The agent of transformation seems to have been the cigar. Jerry inhales deeply from it but hardly releases any smoke, which subtly aids the impression that he is imbibing a kind of intoxicating fuel. This is particularly noticeable in the first axial cut from master to close-up, which is timed to emphasize a deep suck on the cigar as a momentary point of rest (the brief interval between melodic phrases) before he launches into the next pompous pronouncement, accompanied by further pointing. The repetition of this arm gesture conjures a flock of yes-men because of its confident "laziness": he moves from the elbow, rather than from the shoulder. The attitude of disdain also comes across in the way his eyes remain (during the first section) hooded and unresponsive, an effect made noticeable because his mouth and hands are by contrast so mobile and expressive. He tends to fix on a distant mark as if he were looking through those he nominally addresses by pointing. Despite wielding it to engage those around him, however, Jerry's finger, and later his cigar, is not used as a precise pointer but rather more of a flicking baton. The rhythmic pointing-around-the-room gesture is halfway between tallying an inner circle of support and conducting an orchestra. He uses it to keep his minions in line, and in time, with his brassy "voice." Only the voice is not his, and the issuing of directions and utterances that performatively assume power are but Mickey Moused actions to sounds from an unseen elsewhere. The piquancy of this boss-burlesque routine comes from the resulting impression that Jerry is as much puppet as puppeteer.

Binding himself so tightly to the music's phrasing gives Lewis the license to ornament his performance with countless weird and eccentric touches. Consider the extraordinary succession of expressive states accompanying just two melodic phrases roughly halfway through the sketch. Lewis has briefly turned to the side in his swivel chair, presenting a contemptuous profile to the imagined assembly as he flicks ash from the end of his cigar. With two trumpet notes falling a whole tone interval, to which he will mouth something like "Bah–YOU," Jerry snaps from this confident, relaxed posture into a cartoon-surprised cross-eyed expression, suddenly straightening his back and raising his fist to his shoulder on "Baaah—," almost like pulling back for an ineffective ball throw. The hand is then thrown forward into an accusatory pointing gesture on "—YOU," mimed with an oval mouth and angry eyes. This melts, for the briefest split second, into a simpleton smile (tight lips and jutting-out chin) as the hand is retracted, and then fluidly into a sulk as the boss inspects his cigar. This resting pose lasts for less than a second, however. With the arrival of the next jazz phrase, Jerry launches into a flurry of bizarre facial expressions whose moods are almost too quick to catch: a scrunched-up angry expression into long-face surprised into wincing into winking into confused into demonic into crazy, cross-eyed, finally throwing his hands up, mouth wide-open, in an expression that initially looks like surrender but then, with hands abruptly shoved forward, becomes a frustrated stop gesture. All this in approximately six seconds of screen time.

This is as close as comic performance gets to pointillism. The sketch's portrait of the egomaniacal executive is the sum total of all the personae glimpsed in passing: idiot, demon, guru, cynic, tyrant, child, lunatic, ape. The parade of multiple personalities is exemplified by the moment late on when Jerry spins round in his chair and transforms from something like a sports coach persona, whose frantic gesticulations suggest a desperate last-ditch effort to unite the team, to a kind of Halloween spook, arms flung wide, tongue hanging out, on a blast of horns. As he shakes his head in a mad fury, we cut into a close up to witness, for a split-second, Jerry grab at his hair with his fist, in a simian gesture that also disturbingly evokes the distress of a mental patient. Then, moments later, Jerry segues from a fist-shaking toddler tantrum into a "calm down" gesture and a skyward look, performed with a blissful roll of the eyes, as if he were leading the boardroom to some imagined state of nirvana.

Figure 4.4. Jerry Lewis. *The Errand Boy* (Jerry Lewis, 1961).

Figure 4.5. Jerry Lewis. *The Errand Boy* (Jerry Lewis, 1961).

Figure 4.6. Jerry Lewis. *The Errand Boy* (Jerry Lewis, 1961).

Figure 4.7. Jerry Lewis. *The Errand Boy* (Jerry Lewis, 1961).

The number closes with a trumpet solo that Lewis's interpretive dance renders, first, as the giggles of a dope fiend (Jerry waggles his head, as if enjoying a high, and gazes at his smoke), then, to match a series of frenzied runs, as hysterical laughter, eyes popping and head jumping like Woody Woodpecker. As the trumpet settles down, Lewis closes his eyes, and his convulsions evoke self-satisfied amusement. Finally, with the music building to crescendo for the last note, the open laughing smile turns by degrees into a yawn, which morphs, with the baring of teeth, into a roar, capped by a lion's-paw swipe on the final beat. Then we cut back to the master shot to see Jerry snap back into his former errand boy persona, as if awakening from a daydream, with a little chew, blink, and look around. And we too awaken, finding it difficult to process, let alone to recount, the stream of expressions that just issued from across the table.

## "Hot Tub"

The "texture" of comedy is probably more important than its structure. Raymond Durgnat once noted that in order to grasp the appeal of popular music, one needs to

Figure 4.8. Eddie Murphy. *Saturday Night Live* (NBC, 1975–present, S9:E4).

overcome the prime difficulty of the classically-trained music-lover when confronted by a "low" culture musical form (whether pop, jazz, folk or pub). Used to seeking out more or less complex harmonic structures, he does not see that he must here shift his attention away from the harmonic and melodic rigidity to tonal and vocal texture, to the "sound," with its attack, intonation and dynamics. For here most of the emotional charge and subtlety lies. (1964: 55)

It is difficult to imagine a better lesson in the importance of "the sound" in popular music than the instance of a James Brown scream: "Eeeee-oooww!" or "Heee-aay!" Its key qualities are precisely its vocal feel (rough, rasping, gravelly) and the dynamic of its attack (like opening the throttle of a racing car). No musical feature, one feels, could be more inaccessible to traditional harmonic and melodic analysis. Moreover, the impossibility of notation is internally related to its allure (we can't whistle it, capture it: we *need* to hear it again). A similar point could be made about comic performance. The magnetic quality of Eddie Murphy's sunshine grin, for instance, with its wide invitation to revel in his rascal ways or the bravura with which he moves almost bounces with the muscular elasticity of a puppy: these are vital features that a structural gag analysis could never hope to reach.

The "textural" qualities of James Brown and Eddie Murphy are miraculously blended in a classic skit, "Hot Tub," that appeared in 1983 on *Saturday Night Live* (NBC, 1975–present, S9:E4). The financial outlay for this routine must have been substantial. Costs incurred would have included the hiring of what sounds like an eight-piece funk band; an array of stand-ins wielding dummy instruments; a furnished set with performer podiums and ornamental flowers; and, most expensively, the installation of an operational, swirling Jacuzzi bath set into the sound-stage floor. All this was for a two-minute sketch featuring Murphy doing an impersonation. We are asked to entertain that we are watching the lead in to a special kind of talk show, one in which none other than funk legend James Brown invites celebrity guests into a hot tub with him for an interview.

The achievement of the sketch rests squarely on Murphy's full-hearted commitment to the impression. His emulation of Brown's unique performance style is far more tribute than lampoon. After an MC's voice has hailed the arrival of our host and set up the brisk syncopated rhythms of an introductory vamp, Murphy leaps out into the spotlight from behind a parted pair of cabaret lace curtains. To cheers from the studio audience, he offers a celebratory groove, on the spot, showing off his pompadour wig and costume, a lush velvet dressing gown with collar and cuffs that sparkle in the stage lighting, before strutting out with bare feet into the carpeted stage area and turning around to display the letters embossed on the back of the gown: Hot Tub Man #1. This is as much a star entrance for Murphy as it is a send-up of Brown's propensity for plush outfits and self-styled nicknames (Soul Brother Number One, Mr. Dynamite, The Hardest-Working Man in Show Business, etc.). But it also captures, in its combination of playful exhibitionism and the prematch boxer's ritual (the dressing gown, the eyes-down strut), the tension between the sensual and the aggressive in Brown's particular brand of masculinity.

The display of the back of the dressing gown also allows Murphy to spin back around for his intro. The music drops, and he yells his lead-in line into a handheld mic: "Sometime it make me break out in a cold sweat! One, two, three, four . . ." Regardless of the fact that the line makes no particular sense, Murphy's delivery is pitch perfect: the barking tone of the preacher, the rhythm he makes out of the line by making "cold sweat" percussive, and, especially, the drawl he gives to "one, two, three, four." All of these features conjure and recall Brown's performance style, and they are quickly joined by more—that restless bobble on the spot he does while singing, for instance, and the vocal percussion, squeezing in a "Good God" between lines or ending them with "-ah" (as in "Gonna get ya hot-ah").

Murphy's virtuosic skills as a mimic are on display here, but he also occasionally allows the mask to drop. For instance, after having turned to the sections of live band either side of him, in classic James Brown call-and-response mode, to ask whether he should get in the hot tub ("Will it make me sweat?" "Yeah!" "Will it make me wet?" "Yeah!"), he caps the interaction by looking at the audience and, in a controlled way, lets the air out: "Well, well, well." The brief pause is underlined by a close-up of Murphy as he looks out to the studio audience and lets them glimpse the depth of his enjoyment as he keeps them on a piece of string. At which point the vamp kicks in again, and Murphy maintains eye contact with the audience as he segues into a shimmy. This is the art of the tease.

The pastiche song "Hot Tub" (apparently written by Barry Blaustein and David Sheffield, who went on to work with Murphy on *Coming to America* [1988]) recalls various Brown hits, notably "Cold Sweat" (King Records, 1967) and "Hot Pants" (Polydor Records, 1971). And, indeed, with its electric bassline and funky horns, the song could plausibly pass for a James Brown B-side. The opening lines run as follows:

> Hot tub!
> Full of water!
> I say hot tub!
> Very, very hot. Very hot.
> Hot tub! Gonna get ya hot!
> Gonna make ya sweat!

These lyrics are superbly redundant and silly, of course, since they describe only what a hot tub is and does. "Sweat," in a James Brown song, typically invokes masculine torment at the hands of either a seductive or hard-to-get female, while "hot" would be a metaphorical term for a woman's as-if-scalding allure. In the pastiche song, by contrast, the terms are groundingly literal: a jacuzzi is literally "hot"; it may even be "*too* hot"; it will "make you wet" and will literally "make you sweat." Stripped of their more suggestive meanings, the repetition in lines like "Very, very hot. Very hot" evokes not this figure's sexual excitement but his faint-hearted prevarication about lowering his body into a heated bath.

Just when our protagonist seems finally to have mustered the courage to take the plunge, he throws himself down on one knee, evoking the kind of suppliant posture Brown might adopt during a rendition of "Please, Please, Please" (Federal Records, 1956). Wriggling out of his sparkly dressing gown, he turns to the studio audience and yells, with a face that displays brave anguish, that he is "gonna get in the hot tub" (he is now wearing only a pair of gold trunks; the sight of Murphy's semi-naked body is one available pleasure here, a pleasure that is audible in the audience's whoops of delight). With the music pared down to a drumbeat and the lighting down to a single spotlight, the standing musicians crowd in around the hot tub. This conjures a vaguely tribal feel, as if they were hailing their chieftain in the fulfillment of some ritual. But then, seemingly crippled by fear or perhaps finding himself in danger of catching a chill, Murphy starts shuffling on his knees *away* from the hot tub, back toward to the safety of the cabaret curtains. At this point, in a brilliant touch, the MC hurries out with a cape—the same color and with the same emblazoned logo as the dressing gown our man has just cast off!—and drapes it over this frail figure's shoulders, helping him to his feet and steering him toward the exit. The whole business is a parody of a routine in Brown's live concerts whereby, toward the end of an especially intense performance, the singer would feign exhaustion, and a stagehand would put a recovery cape around his shoulders—only for him to throw it off and return to the stage for an encore. The imagery invoked is of boxing or wrestling, with its theater of male suffering, except that, in this context, the swift appearance of the replacement cape pictures the performer as absurdly coddled. It is here that Murphy's fond send-up most cheekily exposes the seam of continuity between the diva and the alpha male.

There is a double layer of pretense here: Eddie Murphy mimics the show routine of James Brown, while "James Brown," in that show routine, presents his audience with a transparently feigned retreat. His hunched demeanor and the conceit that he needs assistance to make it off-stage is a performance within the performance, the mere semblance of defeat by the indefatigable "James Brown." It's a matter of *when* he returns, not *if*. All the while he is led away, Murphy's voice continues to accompany the bare beat—now assisted, bolstered, by rhythmic claps from the audience—still promising, against the visual evidence, that he *will* get in that hot tub. True to his word, just as he reaches the upper podium of the stage, he cries "I can't stand it!" and casts aside the cape—again!—for a heroic comeback, leaping off the podium, back in the direction of the water. There is, in this turnaround, a suggestion of the Christian miracle, of the Evangelist variety, as if the faith exhibited by the audience enacted a laying on of hands, as if the hot tub were some kind of sexy baptismal font. And, lo, in an instant, the hunched, hobbling figure, Old Man Brown, is reborn as a lithe, hip-gyrating, ball of youthful energy: Mr. Dynamite.

He is incredibly lithe, in fact: Murphy works his whole torso as he slinks over the plush stage and back toward the pool. And, *of course*, a James Brown scream—"Heeeaaay!"—is the sound he would make on dipping a toe into intemperate water. With percussive horns hammering out the rhythm, he finds a way to get both feet in the tub—"Good God!"—squirming like an eel as he stands on the first underwater recessed step. And he's *still* not fully submerged. The nature of the funk riff is that it can carry on indefinitely, and Murphy takes full advantage. He, the performer, is so clearly having *fun*—he even allows himself to crack up a little as he repeats the line "Gonna get in the hot tub," as if registering that he knows—that we know—that this sketch is going nowhere other than the endlessly advertised destination.

When—at last—his character settles his body down into the luxuriant bubbles, he yells into the mic: "Don't go away, we'll be right back with more Celebrity Hot Tub!" But of course, it's a fake trail: there will be no return. This is television as perpetual foreplay, endlessly promising whatever is coming up next. The sketch ends by promising an imaginary segment after the commercial break, by means of a deliberately fake-looking doctored photograph of Eddie-as-JB in the hot tub with a D-list celebrity, agony aunt Joyce Brothers. The reference is dated, but you get the idea: incongruent values, awkward proximity . . . car crash TV. But the *SNL* producers evidently realized that the mere suggestion was enough. The format is impossible to imagine: best to keep it that way. Many producers would have been unable to resist milking the premise to death, spinning out an interview format to showcase multiple further impressions. But someone rightly judged that the preamble was the main attraction; that the simplicity of the sketch was its strength; that the music, with its infectious groove, would hold it together; and that Murphy, with his extraordinary confidence and charisma, and by virtue of the precision of his impersonation, would be able to do more with less.

# 5

# Pitched Battles

### "Four Yorkshiremen"

A SIGNIFICANT CLASS OF FINE sketches revolves around the theme of one-upmanship, the attempt to outdo or undercut a rival. Among the many reasons why this would be a conducive theme for sketch comedy is that, as a premise, it can be established quickly and lends itself naturally to escalation. The modern archetype of this format is "Four Yorkshiremen." This sketch is perhaps best known from its various revivals, including the Monty Python stage show released as a concert film, *Live at the Hollywood Bowl* (1982). However, the sketch originally aired on the Python precursor *At Last the 1948 Show* (Associated Rediffusion, 1967, S2:E6) and featured the talents of soon-to-be Pythons Graham Chapman and John Cleese alongside Tim Brooke-Taylor and Marty Feldman as the four Yorkshiremen who take turns to hold forth about how bad things used to be for them.

There is no pain in life, apparently, that cannot be dwarfed by another man's complaint. This is the underlying principle that gives the sketch momentum, as each one-line testimonial, in what passes for a conversation between four Yorkshiremen, seeks to eclipse the preceding claim of hardship and will be in turn belittled. This adheres to a certain commonsense idea that suffering is relative. We habitually grant this idea, for instance, when we inform our kids that *other* children, in malnourished parts of the world, would *leap* at the chance to eat their abandoned broccoli. "Be grateful for small mercies," we tell them. "Count yourself lucky." The

Figure 5.1. Tim Brooke-Taylor, John Cleese, Graham Chapman, and Marty Feldman are the Four Yorkshiremen. *At Last the 1948 Show* (Associated Rediffusion, 1967, S2:E6).

"Four Yorkshireman" sketch takes this received wisdom to a thoroughly unacceptable conclusion. When the First Yorkshireman (Marty Feldman) claims that his father used to thrash him and his siblings with his belt, for instance, the Second Yorkshireman (Graham Chapman) feels able to dismiss this abuse and relabel it as "luxury," on grounds that *his* father apparently used to beat him "about the head and neck with a broken bottle." But that treatment, in turn, is "paradise," according to the Third Yorkshireman (Tim Brooke-Taylor), whose father would nightly carve up his kids with a bread knife.

The joke here is not that poor northern English types like to exaggerate their woes. It does invoke the general stereotype of Yorkshire folk as rugged and proud, but these are very specific types of Yorkshiremen. We are not told how they made their money, but we understand them to be wealthy tycoons of some description. This puts a novel twist on the stereotype of the *nouveau riche*. Instead of gaudily displaying their current level of wealth, they ostentatiously gloat about their level of childhood destitution. The idea is, presumably, to magnify the distance between where they started and where they are now. This is a variant on the fisherman's boast about "the one that got away." But these Yorkshiremen are gloating achievers who are, one suspects, insecure about whether they deserve their reward. This is suggested by the fact that they don't cast doubt on one another's increasingly suspicious claims but appear more concerned with having their own claims accepted in order to maintain a certain standing in the group. The fantasy that crony capitalism is meritocratic is thereby maintained. According to this conspiracy, personal wealth *must* have been attained through hard graft, and the worse you had it to start with, the harder you must have grafted. Fortune can be accorded no role, hence the regular charge "you were lucky" is a kind of character slur. It follows that those who haven't "made it" have been recklessly indolent or else were mollycoddled in their childhood with such extravagances as warm tea.

I have elsewhere offered a chapter-length analysis of "Four Yorkshiremen" with the aim of showing how it makes a virtue of the conditions of its medium, how it is especially "at home" on television (Clayton, 2013). Here I would like to take the opportunity to have another run at it, building on my previous observations but this time focusing more particularly on the artistry of its script and structure. In my earlier account of the sketch, I suggested that it calls us "to survey and savour its emerging shape [and to be] attentive to comic patterns, repetitions and variations" (86). I was especially taken, on that occasion, by the "aesthetic pleasure of the circular return" (86), the way the sketch opens with a symmetrical state of equilibrium, develops into a sequence of escalation, before finally restoring a sense of balance with a return to the opening tableau. I did not have the space, however, in that account (among the various other things I was trying to do) to pay more than fleeting attention to the intricacy with which the scene develops and the richness of imagery it offers. I wish, therefore, to offer some remarks in that direction here. The cleverness of the script still strikes me as a marvel.

Consider, for instance, the progress of this early exchange:

FOURTH YORKSHIREMAN (John Cleese): Who'd have thought, forty years ago, we'd be sittin' here drinking Château de Chasselas.

FIRST YORKSHIREMAN: Aye, we'd have been glad of the price of a cup o' tea, then.

SECOND YORKSHIREMAN: A cup o' cold tea.

FOURTH YORKSHIREMAN: Without milk or sugar.

THIRD YORKSHIREMAN (Marty Feldman): Or tea.

FIRST YORKSHIREMAN: Out a cracked cup, at that.

FOURTH YORKSHIREMAN: We never 'ad a cup. We used to drink out of a rolled-up newspaper.

SECOND YORKSHIREMAN: The best we could manage was to suck on a piece of damp cloth.

The crafting of these lines manufactures two successive lines of intensification. The first escalation of claims, on the subject of a cup of tea (to a British audience, the most basic of everyday items), involves the elimination, by degrees, of all the elements by which tea might provide comfort and sustenance, finally being capped by the impossible removal of its defining condition, in the reference to tea without tea. With the ceiling reached on that particular upcurve, the First Yorkshiremen segues instead into a competition about lowly drinking vessels. A cracked cup is a down-at-heel image but is surpassed by the notion of drinking out of a rolled-up newspaper and that "the *best* we could manage" (i.e., the lordliest, not the most miserable, moment of childhood) was to "suck on a piece of damp cloth." The precision of the script shows itself here: the fact that it is a "piece" of cloth, hence torn, and that it is "damp" rather than "soaked" leads us to imagine it as used and discarded. The combination of that image with a verb that recalls the nursing of infants is what gives the line its understated grotesque quality. One pictures an emaciated Tiny Tim gumming a filthy washrag.

The Dickensian image of urchins seeking damp cloth for sustenance is soon joined by other fantastical imagery—for instance, the image of an enormous extended family living in a "small shoebox in t' middle of road" (like a household of mice). This line of invention, on the topic of childhood homes, starts with John Cleese's Yorkshireman referring to a "tiny tumbledown house with great 'oles in t' roof," a line Cleese embellishes by pointing skywards and repeatedly swiveling his wrist around. The gesture has the curious effect of making the accompanying claim more difficult to imagine (and less creditworthy), since it draws the holes as perfectly circular in appearance, more like the apertures for a pair of massive dome skylights than random ruptures in the roof structure. The sequence of competing claims on this topic of shelter operates under various lines of logic. A single room (for a family of twenty-six) invertedly trumps a house of any description on grounds of space; a hole in the floor is more dangerous than holes in the roof. (The claim that the family were to be found "all 'uddled together in one corner for fear of falling" is another instance of zoomorphic miniaturization: the tense of the continuous past makes them a squirming heap of perpetually terrified creatures.) A corridor is worse than a room, on grounds that at least a room affords privacy, is a place to call one's own. But a corridor is a "palace" compared to living in a "water tank on a rubbish tip" (garbage dump). At least a corridor, one gathers, is dry, sheltered, hygienic, within the orbit of human society. The competing claim systematically reverses each of those benefits.

The "water tank" claim caps the shelter contest and immediately presents the opening move in a new line of development: "Every morning we'd be woke up by having a load of rotting fish dumped all over us." (This came from the man who declared his family were happy *because* they were poor.) The structure of the claim is adapted further by the Yorkshireman who professes to have lived in a rolled-up newspaper in a septic tank: "Every morning we'd 'ave to get up at six, clean out t' rolled-up newspaper, eat a crust of stale bread. Then we'd 'ave to work fourteen 'ours at t' mill, day in, day out, for sixpence a week." This in turn sets the template for the final round of competition on the topic of daily rituals. In this round, however, it is not sufficient for a single variable to be changed. Instead, the intensification must apply to each and every one of its variables. So each successive claim not only rolls back the wake-up time (from 6:00 a.m. to 3:00 a.m. to midnight) but also names a more terrible chore ("clean out t' rolled-up newspaper" to "clean the lake" to "lick t' road clean"), specifies a more revolting breakfast (from "a crust of stale bread" to "a handful of hot gravel" to "a couple of bits of cold gravel"), lengthens the working hours (from fourteen to twenty to twenty-three hours per day at the mill), decreases the wage rate (from sixpence to tuppence to a penny), increases the interval between wage payments (from a week to a month to every four years), *and* closes by recounting, apparently with nothing but gratitude, a more severe regular act of paternal brutality (from "Dad would thrash us to sleep with his belt" to "Dad would beat us about the head and neck with a broken bottle" to "Dad used to slice us in half with a bread knife"). Adding these details together makes each reported state of affairs not just marginally worse but *exponentially* worse. Moreover, the bar starts high—it doesn't seem possible to *imagine* a worse scenario than the Third Yorkshireman's report of living in a shoe box, having to lick the road clean, being butchered by the father, and so on. And yet the sketch is able to deliver one further "raise," a masterpiece of self-contradiction:

> FOURTH YORKSHIREMAN: We used to get up in morning, at 'alf past ten at night, 'alf an 'our *before* we'd gone to bed, eat a lump of poison, work twenty-nine hours at mill for ha'penny a lifetime, come home and each night Dad would strangle us and dance about on our graves.

Waking before sleeping, poison as nourishment, working for longer than a day each day, collecting your wage only after your death, being murdered every night: each of its components is brilliantly impossible.

The project of working variants on the day-in-the-life "template" is an extraordinary comic device that seems to emerge naturally from the comedic conversation because so many elements of its premise have already been established (e.g., the "rule" that these men will take turns to share childhood recollections, the uncomplaining attitude with which they recount such stories, the credulity with which each claim will demand to be received, and so on). By this stage, we are able to anticipate not only that each subsequent claim will be a report of more severe conditions but also the syntactical form it is likely to take. Remarkably, however, the sketch resists becoming an ossified ritual. One reason for this is the mastery of rhythm and variation in the construction of dialogue. Just as we reach the threshold of becoming accustomed to a particular tempo, the rhythm changes. For example: "'Ouse? You were lucky." is succeeded by "Room? You were lucky" so that when Marty Feldman's Yorkshireman says "Corridor?" we might naturally expect it to be followed by another "You were lucky." But with that, the rhythm would have started to flag, the sketch dissolving into a tired exchange of catchphrases. So instead it is followed by "Oh, I used to dream of livin' in a corridor. That would ha' been a palace to us," which introduces a complete rhythmic change and draws a line under that section. A few lines later, Tim Brooke-Taylor's Yorkshireman seems to start it all off again: "You were lucky to have a lake: there were over a hundred and fifty of us living in a small shoebox in t' middle o' road." But rather than the retort being "Shoebox? You were lucky," or "You were lucky to have a shoebox," either of which would have seemed lazily mechanical, Feldman throws back a follow-up question:

FELDMAN: CARDBOARD BOX?

BROOKE-TAYLOR: Aye.

FELDMAN: Aye, you were lucky.

The main function of this request for clarification is to break the pattern of strict alternation, keeping us on our toes. Only second to this function is the purpose of highlighting the deeper logic that cardboard is the lofty cousin of paper (a material that more readily gets soggy and soiled: "a rolled-up newspaper in a septic tank" is next in the chain of abodes).

Just as important as the rhythm is the baroque stylization of the script. Giving each statement a form and purpose that is known in advance is what allows for this elaborate ornamentation, the fleeting appearance of details that tease our cognitive, imaginative, and even sensory faculties. The idea of eating a handful of hot gravel for breakfast, for example: you can almost feel it scalding your palms, and burning and scratching your esophagus. The reply posits that *cold* gravel is even worse, presumably on the logic that, as a breakfast item, cold porridge is the poor man's hot porridge. And somehow you can imagine the children foraging for gravel in the road outside their shoebox, dreaming of the chance to heat it through and make it more digestible. Likewise, living in a lake. What are we picturing here? Fully submerged underwater, a family in scuba gear or sitting and shivering in its stony shallows? What manner of threat must this family be under such that they are forced to live *in* it, not beside it? And how does this tally with the excessive house pride that dictates that the children must rise at 3:00 am to "clean the lake"? Does that suggest the collection of floating detritus in the dark cold hours before daybreak? But that would be more "tidying" than "cleaning." In the context of home maintenance, "cleaning" implies scrubbing, wiping, polishing—so perhaps the Sisyphean task of sweeping a layer of silt from the lakebed each morning, piling it up on the shore. For what purpose? In case the neighbors visit? The suggestion seems solid until you venture to grasp it—at which point the sense evaporates. The humor resides in the fact that we find ourselves trying to conceive the inconceivable, to picture the unthinkable.

## "Price War"

If capitalism is a battleground, the TV commercial is where the bombardment begins. Mock-advertisements are a staple of sketch comedy for a range of reasons. Most obviously, ads and movie trailers are typically brief in duration, which means they can be spoofed from start to finish and allow the make-believe that you are watching the real thing. In addition, an image-rich mock-advertisement sketch can offer a useful comic item to place between more dialogue-heavy skits (perhaps even mimicking the way broadcast commercials are themselves "filler" material) and allow for variation in type and pace of sketch. Moreover, due to their (obnoxious) ubiquity and the need for a promotional message to be succinct and (irritatingly) direct, TV adverts of various kind tend to have a highly distinctive iconography or look, as well as a recognizably typical narrative and rhetorical procedure. This, in turn, makes them readily available for parody. Finally, and often most importantly, an advert-based sketch, unlike a situational sketch where the motivations of characters need some exposition, comes with a simple, ready-made motivation: the

Figure 5.2. Eric Wareheim is about to strike Tim Heidecker. *Tim and Eric Awesome Show, Great Job!* (Abso Lutely Productions, S4:E3, 2009).

company behind the commercial wants to show its product or brand in a (perhaps cloyingly, perhaps aggressively) positive light. The satirical opportunity therefore presents itself to undermine that effort, perhaps exposing, through the gaps of its advertisement idiom, the shoddiness or impracticality of the item being touted or the vacuity of the values being espoused.

"Price War," from *Tim and Eric Awesome Show, Great Job!* (Abso Lutely Productions, S4:E3, 2009), takes full advantage of these opportunities. The show has a distinctively astringent tone, typically peppering its brand of cringe comedy with bizarre, often inexplicable, details. Its stars and creators, Tim Heidecker and Eric Wareheim, in this and other collaborations, regularly offer fake segments of TV broadcast material, including news items, celebrity chat, science programs, and cookery instruction shows, alongside spoof advertisements. The particular ad form being spoofed here is the very American phenomenon of the local broadcast commercial promoting a nearby shopping outlet, salesroom, or dealership. One trope of this genre is the appearance of the business proprietor himself, walking the parking lot and inviting viewers to "Come on over!" The casting of the actual owner in the role is presumably meant to assure viewers that he or she (typically he) is successful, self-reliant, and ordinary, a figure "like you" who is therefore to be trusted on quality and/or value ("or your money back"), as you, the viewer, might well expect yourself to be trusted. Typical visual features of this type of production include an abundant use of bold graphics, designed to inject some liveliness into the affair (perhaps overcompensating for washed-out color, poor lighting, and uncharismatic performances), and a tendency to overload the image with redundant text set in gaudy typeface. Then there is the characteristic behavioral style of the onscreen figures, whose amateur delivery offers some combination of the stilted and the shouty, and who carry out the publicity stunts of their big TV role with a mannered, near-feverish enthusiasm.

Given some attention to detail, these are relatively easy targets for the would-be parodist. "Price War" caricatures all of the above traits with a pleasing precision, but what makes the sketch more successful an achievement than the standard already well-known comedic local-ad spoof is its abstraction of the form through the introduction of several unique and surreal elements. First, the advert highlights not a range of products for sale but, far more indeterminately, a range of prices that can, in some nebulous sense, be paid, as if the transaction itself were the desired outcome rather than any product. Second, the ad is imagined not as the univocal message it most usually is, but as the site of a battleground between competing interests. In brief, we understand the owners of two separate companies—Tim Heidecker, president of Tim's Discount Prices (played by Tim Heidecker) and Eric Wareheim of Eric's Premium Prices (played by Eric Wareheim)—to be vying for customers by repeatedly hijacking and counterhijacking one another's sales pitch.

Beyond the wacky premise, the sketch is interspersed with myriad wild details delivered at a pace that bequeaths a distinctively manic feel. Some of these details seem designed almost to avoid recognizability on a first viewing, or at least to take advantage of a delay before they penetrate our consciousness. The very first line of the sketch, for example, has Tim Heidecker turn to the camera to introduce himself. But what he *actually* says is: "Hi, me mo mo Tim Heidecker and welcome to Discount Prices." Come again? The rhythm and tonality of the spiel is so familiar that even gibberish can pass under the radar.

The rapid pace of the sketch's unfolding is justified by the fact that local advertisements, trying to make the most of a tight budget, typically seek to cram in as many selling points as possible within the given time frame. Heidecker's opening patter ("I've got 1.99! I've got 7.99! I've got 16.99!"), for instance, is so keen to get across the range of available "prices" that he is digitally cloned, a new image of Tim Heidecker appearing onscreen for each sales point, and the sound editing matches this duplication by having each exclamation by a newly spawned Tim overlap with the sound of the previous one (e.g., "I've got 7.99!" begins before "I've got 1.99!" has even finished). This is recognizable as the kind of device that might credibly be deployed by TV advertising to convey an idea of warehouse overflow. Nothing is undersold: with the announcement of each price, a spiky red graphic text box containing the word "CHEAP!" is pasted at an angle across the screen. The rate gets quicker as Tim shouts a string of further numbers: "Fourteen! Eleven! Two Forty-Nine!" With the calling out of each price, the salesman's image leaps quickly and successively across the green-screened parking lot until "Two Forty-Nine!" is delivered in a medium close-up, straight to camera. Then, with a dead-eye expression, Heidecker turns his head away from the camera and says, "Three." The weirdness of this detail is principally the consequence of (deliberate) misdirection in delivery: Heidecker projects the word, with an insistently fat "th" on "th-ree," slightly downwards, offscreen right, as if he had momentarily forgotten where the camera is placed. The oddness is also partly the effect of anticlimax, the final number being arbitrarily a little higher, rather than lower, than the previous number in what had seemed to be a descending series (14 > 11 > 2.49 < 3). A palpable sense of deflation, like the air squealing out of a balloon, also arises because the background chintzy music that had been accompanying the advert suddenly halts, an instant prior to Tim saying the number, isolating the utterance on the soundtrack. Briefly abandoned by the advert's supporting rhetoric, our store manager distractedly barks a meaningless number into empty space: "THREE."

The sketch takes a yet weirder turn with the arrival of Eric Wareheim, who steps into shot and appears to strike Tim Heidecker, causing him to disintegrate. Aside from the suddenness of the intrusion, this also introduces a confusion of diegetic levels. The shot of Heidecker dancing outside his Discount Store was already a blatant composite shot, combining studio footage of the performer with a green-screen backdrop of the parking lot. When Wareheim appears, the consistency of lighting and angle initially seems to place him in the same performance space as Heidecker. However, when he elbows his rival, Heidecker falls back like a cardboard cut-out and breaks into a pile of pixelated pieces. At the very point of "contact" between them, therefore, Wareheim is situated in a different space from Heidecker, and at a temporal remove (assuming the postproduction effects necessary to create the visual effect of smashing his rival have taken a little time to prepare). Although we hardly have the opportunity, in the moment, to gather all this and bring it to mind, it is indicative of the way the sketch makes continuous demands upon us to reorient ourselves in relation to where we are and what we are seeing.

Wareheim has not really clouted his rival but has merely unleashed the first in a series of acts of virtual violence. The disintegration of Heidecker is, we gather, a graphic visualization of a turn of phrase: Wareheim accompanies his action by declaring that "Tim's prices shatter to the ground." This is, however, a curious wording. The poetic idiom "shatter to the ground" is familiar enough when applied to something brittle, but it seems to lack connection with the concept of "prices." Similarly, when Heidecker reappears onscreen shortly thereafter, he does so by apparently hatching out of (the image of) Wareheim's head and telling his rival to "lay an egg." The context suggests it means something like "get lost" or "take a hike," but it's an unknown turn of phrase. Each of these alien expressions is matched to a virtual action and duplicated in text on the screen. Yet for all this reiteration, the comic strategy is for these traded slogans to defy easy assimilation, either by being readily explicable or all-too-obviously nonsensical. They *barely* make sense.

The same goes for the sketch as a whole. It is difficult to get any rational purchase on the concept of selling *prices*. You just have to go with it. Similarly, while it is possible to credit that a business owner might, in an ad campaign, rerun a sequence from a rival's previous ad campaign, only to interject, virtually insert himself, and undercut the claim, it is considerably more challenging to imagine that the rival would then, in response, screen both a segment of his original ad *and* a segment of his competitor's counterclaim before injecting once again—and so on, back and forth, adding cumulatively to each successive interruption for more than twenty rounds of advertisement tennis. Tim hatches out of Eric's head to vaunt some further price reductions; Eric bursts through that image as if through a brick wall to announce that "Tim buys his prices from China," whereas his are "American-made"; no sooner has that claim been made than Tim bursts onto the screen riding a horse and decapitates his rival; Eric appears to hook a piece of text ("$1.19") from Tim's advert using a fishing rod, yanks it out of shot, declares that he won't feed it to his family, and throws it in a river; a gunshot wound appears on Eric's chest, and we find Tim wielding a rifle and claiming that Eric has a smelly crotch; Eric's face, attached to the body of a seagull, slides onscreen to declare, "Discount prices are for the birds," following this up with a claim that Tim has "crap prices" while standing next to a sign reading "¢89" apparently made out of feces.

The grotesque, acidic feel of all this comes partly from the combination of violence with crude sexual and scatological reference, but it also arises from the unsettlingly malleable image. Moreover, the pace quickens, and the sketch's sadism grows more extreme as the counterclaims escalate. Tim warns viewers not to go near Eric as "He'll rape ya," using a matter-of-fact tone of voice that makes it sound like a certainty ("*He*'ll rape ya"), a claim reiterated in lurid pink text. But there is no time for this outrageous charge to be substantiated as Eric performs a virtual hit-and-run, whizzing past in a convertible and throwing Tim's prone body over the hood; Tim retorts by exploding Tim's car with an air-to-surface missile and, from the cockpit of a fighter plane, broadcasting the allegation that Eric is a "compulsive masturbator"; Eric freezes his rival, brands his body with the word "LIAR!," and slices his head off with a single karate chop. The whole thing culminates in a frenetic montage that reaches fever pitch as each salesman furiously barks out his message and superimposes himself on the other, the impossibly rapid alternation of images finally bringing about a cosmic explosion. A spot of "healthy competition" between local businesses has caused the destruction of the galaxy. That's *one* way to end a sketch.

## "Singing Contest"

Stanley Cavell has referred to the "repetitive little deaths" we inflict and incur in our daily lives, those countless small-scale wounds to one's character that go unremarked, dwarfed in size, though not in number, by the horror and violence of events reported in news headlines. These are the mental injuries that derive from interpersonal negligence, from the failure to acknowledge that people around us have inner lives that are sensitive to our behavior, and from the habit of swallowing our own hurt feelings. Cavell wonders if what he calls "the laboratory of film"—by extension moving image media more widely—might help us see this phenomenon more clearly, that

Figure 5.3. Sally Phillips sings, and Doon Mackichan ignores. *Smack the Pony* (Fremantle Media, S1:E1, 1999).

in our slights of one another, in an unexpressed or disguised meanness of thought, in a hardness of glance, a willful misconstrual, a shading of loyalty, a dismissal of intention, a casual indiscriminateness of praise or blame—in any of the countless signs of skepticism with respect to the reality, the separateness, of another—we run the risk of suffering, or dealing, little deaths every day." (2005: 340)

Cavell labels such acts of everyday carelessness "signs of skepticism" because they typically involve a disavowal that people around us are reached by our behavior, that they too have inner lives that are sensitive to our dealings. One might wonder if such a skeptical disavowal is made all too easy in the many social situations where directly looking at one another, into one another's eyes, is, for one reason or another, culturally unacceptable. The most obvious example would be passengers on subway trains, although the taboo reaches into many areas of nonintimate social life. If, as is often said, "the eyes are the window of the soul," we see in such a case how a social convention ostensibly founded on the granting of privacy could actually foster a denial, or at least forgetfulness, of one another's humanity. In combination with this taboo on direct looking, there is, adding to the problem, the frequent compulsion to *cloak* personal expressions, whether to adhere to a rule of minimizing emotional disclosure in certain situations (e.g., among nonintimate colleagues at work) or otherwise out of fear of one's feelings being caught "out in the open." The fact that feelings and motives are so often cloaked can exacerbate a sense that we surely all have, from time to time, that other people are difficult to read, hence difficult to reach; certainly, a sense that other people think we are.

All of this might sound a million miles from comedy, and yet it chimes precisely with a superlative British TV sketch from the female-led troupe of *Smack the Pony* (Fremantle Media, S1:E1, 1999). Two employees are occupying themselves during a work break. The younger woman (Sally Phillips), looking through photos and monthlies, begins to sing along to a song on the radio, at first absent-mindedly, then with more purpose. Her colleague (Doon Mackichan) then joins in, or rather takes over, warbling stretches of the song in a display of her superior singing voice. The first employee strains to out-sing her rival but gets frustrated and finally lets out a scream. Instead of confronting her colleague, she blames it on a paper cut inflicted from a glossy magazine.

The two characters, colleagues who are not (we take it) friends, seem bound to a code of conduct, and basis for esteem, that actively inhibits the free exchange of looks and the open disclosure of feelings.

The junior colleague's apparently sudden inclination to share her melancholy mood with her acquaintance is therefore "covered" by means of an expression—raising her voice to join in with a sad song on the radio—that could (if called out on it) be excused as a merely blithe or unconscious singalong. In turn, this indirectness of expression allows the senior colleague to misconstrue the singing as some kind of status claim and "slap down" her colleague by singing it better than she had.

The crucial factor here is that the whole scene is presented in a single, unbroken take, keeping both characters in frame throughout and thereby permitting us uninterrupted access to their body language. The long take allows us, for instance, to notice the junior colleague's fleetingly wounded expression as she makes a series of cautious looks in the direction of her shame-inflicting neighbor, pained glances accentuated by purple eye shadow and dark liner. Being able to observe the senior colleague throughout, we are also placed to gather (without it being picked out for us) that her motive for repudiation comes from a position of personal repression and bitterness, belied by the sweetness of her reed. Similarly, when the junior colleague returns to the fray, joining in with the song once again, we can observe in her expression that this has now become a matter of pride, a battle for recognition, even as she is conscious that it opens her up for further rebuke. Each woman strives to appear resolutely unimpressed, to deny the affirmation that is sought. We perceive especially in the junior colleague how much labor it takes to affect nonchalance and to suppress any potentially flattering show of envy.

"Singing Contest" allows us access to this realm of quotidian struggle, with its perpetual threat of mortification, because of the everyday setting and its refusal to escalate into all-out farce. It is a noteworthy achievement, in fact, to have devised a sketch that is entirely rooted in the everyday (contrast, for example, the *Key and Peele* sketch "Awkward Conversation," discussed in the introduction, which starts with an ordinary situation but evolves it into something altogether more fantastical). The workplace locale is established by panning across a stack of cardboard (boxes awaiting assembly) and over to the two women. On the soundtrack, the banging of tools and the familiar squeak of shoes on vinyl flooring gives the space as a warehouse. However, we find the women dressed in identical work uniforms, which suggests they are customer-facing employees. This yields two further insights: first, that this warehouse is for them a kind of back room where they go to have their coffee breaks but that is not really *their* space; second, that they are hardly prized employees. They apparently have no distinct staff social area aside from the little makeshift space produced by two basic plastic chairs and some temporarily placed cardboard boxes, one of which is used for a table between them, another of which provides a footstool: small comforts. In turn, from the fact that heavy (filled) boxes, presumably containing saleable goods, are available for foot-rest purposes we might surmise that this stock is not going anywhere fast. In other words, this place is not only a back room but a backwater. All of this rapidly intuited information lays the ground for the sketch's emotional keynote, the feeling of being unseen and unvalued.

The contrasting physiques of Doon Mackichan and Sally Phillips are put shrewdly to work here to suggest a power dynamic and convey their relationship. It is Doon Mackichan's long legs that are using the box as a footstool, implying a confident maturity and territorial dominance as she works a crossword puzzle. Her seated posture is angular, and the profile view brings out the performer's potential to appear stern. By contrast, Sally Phillips is curled up, like an infant animal, as she cycles through a stack of photos. Her knees are up and together to allow her to use her lap as the resting place for a magazine and the photos' folder. An important detail in suggesting her meekness is the fact that she keeps these items to herself rather than laying them out on a nearby box. Phillips's high forehead and sad eyes confirm her character as an introvert, and one gathers she is new to the workplace. It's difficult to resist the inference, from the combination of her age and her wistful looking at photos, that she has just returned from a postuniversity gap year of traveling, and now finds herself depressingly back in the "real world," in whatever small town this happens to be. That would suggest a bleak reading of the conspicuous color match between her tousled dyed-blonde hair and the mousy, straw-textured blonde wig sported by the older-looking Mackichan: its more "mature" style implies that the frosty older woman is what the sensitive younger woman will, in time, become.

Their body language makes plain they are acquaintances through work, not friends outside it. They are sitting together but not to spend time with one another. As Phillips absorbs herself in the tokens of her memories and Mackichan attends to her crossword puzzle, no looks or words are exchanged. Amid the intermittent sounds of the warehouse, we hear a radio broadcasting what we are likely to recognize as the piano lead-in to a verse of Harry Nilsson's "Without You." It's important that its timbre is tinny, and its volume does not at first surpass the background sounds of the warehouse, not just because this underlines the idea that these are undervalued employees (no high-quality sound system for you), but also for the idea of the radio as providing aural wallpaper, to cover the silence of noninteraction rather than to provide entertainment. The early sound mix gives no hierarchical distinction between music and noise (music is potentially just more noise). This is significant for the later implication that things are getting out of joint, when background becomes foreground, and the singing voice assumes a prominence that is inappropriate (inappropriate in the sense of uncalled for rather than outrageous or taboo: singing in a warehouse is not like singing in a library).

The singalong starts innocently enough with Phillips softly accompanying some lyrics, joining in halfway through the line "No I can't forget tomorrow / When I think of all your sorrow." From her action of ruefully looking through printed photographs, we infer a mood match: she comes in on "can't forget," which suggests the function of photographs as memory prompts (recalling that gap year, perhaps). At any rate, the singing is absentminded, prompted by internal reflection, since she dips in and out of the song without self-consciousness. She is not, at this point, fully present in the room; she is back where the photos were taken with the companions they show.

Moreover, she is not (yet) performing. That she is singing for herself alone, not projecting for others, is conveyed by the fact that she uses her southern English accent, which gives a short "o" to "sorrow" (instead of the American Harry Nilsson's "sa-rrow") and a long "u-oh" on the end word of "let you go." Phillips's exaggeration of this parochial accent, where the lingering on "go" becomes almost a "gurr," could raise an expectation that we are about to see an observational-comedy sketch about a familiar kind of annoying workmate, one who selfishly violates the precious peace of break time. Accordingly, we check in on Mackichan's response. To our surprise, however, there's no obvious sign of irritation. The standard choice here would have been to cut in to a reverse-angle close-up of an eye roll or a huff as Mackichan strains to tolerate a bothersome colleague. Instead, the sketch refuses both analytical editing and gestural sign posting. Is Mackichan's brief raising of a hand to her temple a symptom of a will to blot out this distraction from her crossword? Does she remain undisturbed, or does she merely wish to *appear* undisturbed (unbothered, unimpressed)? Is the slight outtake of breath a sigh of frustration or simply forbearance in the face of a tricky puzzle (moving on to a different clue)? From this vantage, with Mackichan in profile, it's not easy to tell. By withholding a clarification of Mackichan's attitude at this early stage, the sketch puts us into a mode of viewing where we must scan surface behavior, search for what it might betray.

The structure of the sketch is bound to the structure of the ballad, in particular the song's alternation between ruminative verse and melodramatic refrain. Putting away her photos into their folder, Phillips finds herself taken by the chorus lead-in, slapping her leg with the envelope to supply a percussive fill, bobbing her head back and forth, pursing her lips in attentiveness to its rhythm as if momentarily imagining herself as the band's drummer. Immediately, we recognize that, having put some feeling into the verse and propelled by the momentum of this lead-in, Phillips now finds herself committed to belting out the chorus. This discovery manifests the first sign of self-consciousness in the character: a stuttering little pause and blink as she navigates a major sixth interval. The hand holding the pack of photos hovers in midair for a moment as she searches for the transition note, sliding awkwardly into pitch (or thereabouts) from "Can't" up in the direction of "live." Without acknowledging her colleague, she seems for the first time conscious of her presence and the bounds of workplace propriety, which surely cannot permit a wholehearted rendition of the song. As if to redeem this momentary overreaching and to stress the casualness of her commitment, even as she carries on singing, she reaches for a glossy magazine. Flipping through its pages with feigned attention allows her to continue her recital while effectively seeming blasé. But true feeling creeps back in again. When she sings "Can't *give* any more," she closes her eyes on "give" and juts her head forward with heartfelt emphasis, the emotional surge disguised only by the nonchalant act of folding over the magazine spine to inspect a feature.

Throughout all of this, the senior work colleague has been silently attending to her crossword, occasionally chewing on a pen or rehearsing some letters on her puzzle, for all the world absorbed. Maintaining a two shot, the camera has undertaken a gradual zoom, cropping the wider environment of the warehouse to frame the pair more tightly. One subtle and effective consequence of the progressive shift in focal length is to contract the void between the two characters, so they appear increasingly, more uncomfortably, pressed together in the space. So far it has been Sally Phillips who, due to her more ostensive behavior and the angle of view that favors her full face, has principally called for our notice. Mackichan, in side profile, could seem the background character. So it comes as something of a surprise when the senior colleague suddenly takes up the chorus with a commitment and vocal proficiency that markedly outshines—and is, we have to judge, *meant* to outshine—her co-worker.

Mackichan's delivery is set to highlight every feature that Phillips's voice relatively lacks: strength, precision, clarity of timbre, and a "professional" American country accent ("can't" in "can't live" pronounced "cay-nt"). Where Phillips's voice was strained and uncertain, Mackichan's is bright and sure. While Phillips struggled for pitch, Mackichan performs the melodic arc of "can't live" with a confident *vibrato*. Closed eyes, mobile shoulders, and a little shake of the head confirm her mastery of (the conventions of) properly "emotional" delivery. She is, in fact, ridiculously overcompetent. Yet, at the same time, her lower body remains pointedly unmoved, just to confirm the message that this comes so easily to her.

Throughout the solo, her pen hovers over her magazine as if she were still really considering the crossword. In a delightfully droll gesture, timed to coincide with the final word of the chorus, Mackichan puts ink to paper to fill in a letter on her puzzle and then raises the pen to her forehead as if to mark a victory. End of round 1.

Finding herself sung down, Phillips's initial response is to throw a resentful glance in her neighbor's direction, the first time either character has cast a direct look at the other. She tries to cultivate indifference, briefly feigning study of a page in her magazine before taking a sip from her can of cola, the movement of which provides cover for another sideways glance. But puppy-dog eyes unmistakably show she has been stung by this karaoke incursion. Then the expression hardens, forming pursed lips, and a forward stare to ground confirms surrender will not be an option. The next verse begins, and we witness some emergency preparations. Trying to feel her way back into the song, odd syllables are mouthed before a resumption is launched—awkwardly, midline, out of sync: "—guess that's just the way the story goes." The lyrics may speak of resignation, but a scrunch of the nose on "just," almost a snarl, affects hard-bitten resilience. The adoption of a gruff American accent now is a blatant attempt to reinvent herself as an indie singer, making a virtue of vocal imprecision by draping it in husky tones. The contrast is meant to signal that her rival's vocal embellishments were overly fancy, inauthentic. Unfortunately, her eagerness to face down her rival spoils the devil-may-care persona. At the end of the line, Phillips shoots a look at her colleague, who has returned to the pretense of immersion in her puzzle, which is both a check for response and a display of sultry aggression (sidelong glance, clenched teeth). But now, perhaps annoyed by her rival's lack of response, the upstart singer is thrown off her game and fluffs the start of the next line, finding her feet again on "smile but in your eyes your sorrow shows." To provoke at least some kind of reaction, Phillips ramps up the performance with a theatrical grimace on "eyes." Most absurd and desperate of all, at the end of the line, she pinches and waggles the skin on her throat, as if externally manipulating her windpipe to force a tremolo on "shows." Mackichan calmly answers by rounding off the verse, with a devastating show of finesse, pitching it two octaves higher just because she *can*. "Yes, it shows" is the key line, with the implication that the senior employee has seen and noted her colleague's effort. After an instant's overlap, Phillips clams up and sourly glares at her magazine. Meanwhile, Mackichan closes her eyes in rapture, head rolling around her shoulders, ornamenting the line with the grace of a choirgirl. Having put the verse to bed, she returns to her crossword and again fills in some squares.

But the junior colleague is not yet ready to concede defeat. Tinny piano chords signal the chorus is imminent, and we witness the junior colleague steeling herself for another go. But she misses her cue and rejoins too late, throwing her voice into a screech when she goes for the high note. Finding herself disastrously out of vocal range, she attempts a recovery by effecting a falsetto, trying to carry it off by emulating the proud face and clipped diction of a classical vocalist, while simultaneously straining to disguise its exertion by browsing the pages of her magazine, even though the volume of accompaniment is now way past anything that could be mistaken for casual singalong. In rejoinder, Mackichan goes full soprano: she throws her head back and belts out the song with maximum force, supplementing the performance with operatic mannerisms, expressive head shakes, and stagey blinks to complete the impression of virtuosity. Phillips, seeing that she cannot compete in this register, turns out a furious scream. In self-consciousness, it quickly subsides into a throat shout, and she pretends to nurse a finger. "Paper cut," she reports, and the camera pans away.

"Paper cut" is not exactly a punchline, but it's a fitting way of rounding off the sketch. The junior colleague makes the claim as an attempt to back out of the competition with dignity. Yet the way she delivers it is like a child "being brave" to gain the attention of a parent or teacher. It is, notably, the first time that her senior colleague has been drawn into looking at her directly. If "paper cut" denies by trivializing whatever genuine sorrow the song was originally helping to soothe, it achieves for the first time an acknowledgment of her existence, however fleeting and scornful. It is as if there were, after all, some truth to the lyric "Can't live . . . if living is without you," even if the "you" is an unsympathetic colleague. The sketch pictures a form of social life governed by the need to be affirmed, recognized—above all, as in the contemporary myth of the talent scout and the parable of the TV singing competition, *discovered*—a life of noisy efforts to quell quiet desperation.

# Conclusion

## The Rhetoric of Humor

EARLIER IN THIS BOOK, I observed the deficiencies of what has traditionally passed for comic theory—the explanation for "why we laugh"—as a tool for understanding what makes something funny. The subsequent chapters were intended to demonstrate the possibility of getting to grips with the substance of comic instances directly, that is, without the need for a guiding hypothesis. What I offered for each of the dozen or so sketches discussed in this book was a description of concrete details and an articulation of how I understood these details, their implications, and effects, to be working comedically, in synthesis with one another.

These accounts are unlikely to *persuade* anyone who is inclined to find one of these sketches unfunny that it is, in fact, funny. Hopefully, someone who is already inclined to be amused by the material will gain from my account a more vivid sense of how it achieves this effect. However, I would tend to agree with Ted Cohen, in his book on jokes, when he observes that "you cannot show that [a] joke is an instance of something that *must* be acknowledged as funny, as you might show that an argument is an instance of valid reasoning" (1999: 29, italics added). Importantly, this does not mean that any attempt to say how humor works is merely "subjective," in the sense in which that word is sometimes used, to imply that any effort to interpret and evaluate art is redundant. A truly private joke, like a private language, is an impossibility. Humor is always shared. Each of the comic instances I have discussed in this book has been, and continues to be, found funny by many people, and it is wildly unlikely that they are all finding it funny in unique and idiosyncratic ways.

To call something funny is to say that it appeals to the funny bone. No doubt a particular kind of funny bone—but it is the nature of the "appeal" that matters here. The title of this book calls it the art of humor, but it could otherwise be described as comic rhetoric. Notwithstanding his reductive definition of comedy (as the imitation of people who are "worse than the average" [as quoted in Morreall, 1986: 14]), Aristotle can be helpful for thinking through the different dimensions of the "appeal" of comedy. Thinking principally of political oratory, but offering categories that would pertain to a more expansive notion of rhetoric, Aristotle identified three modes of persuasive utterance:

> Of the modes of persuasion furnished by the spoken word there are three kinds. The first kind depends on the personal character of the speaker [*ethos*]; the second on putting the audience into a certain frame of mind [*pathos*]; the third on the proof, or apparent proof, provided by the speech itself [*logos*]. (2004: 7)

These three kinds of persuasion (*ethos, pathos, logos*) might be thought of as interlinked aspects of rhetorical address. As it applies to oratory, *ethos* would describe the appeal to conviction through personal trustworthiness and group affiliation. *Pathos* refers to the appeal to emotion, the effort to *move* listeners towards agreement (for instance, by heightening the poignancy of an anecdote, or by deploying language in a way that generates a persuasively satisfying rhythm, such as the "rule of three" when listing positive attributes). Finally, *logos* refers to the appeal to reason, the attempt to convince an audience of a point by presenting evidence in a certain way. Any instance of persuasive speech is likely to involve all three kinds of appeal.

Each of Aristotle's categories has, I argue here, an analogue in comic rhetoric. Distinguishing between them might help us from becoming fixated on a single aspect of comedy and hopefully allow for a more holistic assessment of how something is funny. The following sections will outline these three types or aspects of humorous appeal, recalling examples discussed previously in the book to serve as illustrations.

### *Logos*

The *logos*, or logical-conceptual dimension, of a comic instance would be its animating ideas and contrasts and how they are presented. A comedy sketch, for instance, is typically organized around a central comic conceit, as we found perhaps most vividly with the "thought experiment" type of sketch, where we are asked to entertain the logic and potential consequences of a fanciful idea, such as the suggestion that a gorilla might learn to speak English fluently ("Gerald the Gorilla," discussed in chapter 3). The conceit may be gradually unveiled, as in the dawning upon us, in "Spiffington Manse" (chapter 2), that there is too much furniture and too little space, or it may be given to us in a nutshell at the opening of the sketch for subsequent elaboration, as in the so-lucid-it's-dreamlike presentation of the premise of Buñuel's "Toilet Party" sequence (also chapter 3). The internal logic of the scenario may be entirely available to us, and almost credible, as in the notion that James Brown might host a jacuzzi-based talk show, or the sense of it may remain deliberately obscure throughout, a challenge to rationalization, as in the idea of a discount store that offers a range of "prices" but no tangible products, in "Price War" (chapter 5).

The *logos* of humor would also include the articulation and development of comic contrasts. "Swimming Pool" (chapter 1), for example, establishes and then complicates the contrast between self-gratification and self-effacement, egotism and altruism. At first, Andy's glottal insistence—"I wanna geddin!," echoing cavernously around the municipal swimming baths—suggests an insatiable demand for instant pleasure, in contrast to the excessive procedural caution with which Lou consults the pool attendant. However, Lou's displayed commitment to his duties, as he prattles away, begins to smack of egotism; conversely, Andy's devil-may-care pleasure seeking soon becomes a race to conceal his true nature, to return to the wheelchair unnoticed, and thereby, as if altruistically, to allow Lou to continue in the caregiving role on which his identity is staked. The relationship between ostensible opposites is far knottier, more intricate, varied, and unfolding than the reductive notion of "incongruity" would suggest. The apparent simplicity of the action belies the density of comic suggestion that I have found, throughout this book, to be a crucial factor in what makes things funny.

Attending to the *logos* dimension of comedy means trying to order the "crush of thoughts" that humor invariably arouses. We encountered this when we considered (in the introduction) the choice of a parrot, of all creatures, for the dead pet in the Monty Python sketch, along with the cluster of associations set off by the use of the word "deceased." We considered a different type of density in the performance of Jerry Lewis, setting off mental fireworks as he cycles madly through a succession of personae in the boardroom ("idiot, demon, guru, cynic, tyrant, child, lunatic, ape," chapter 4). We found parody particularly apt to engineer a kind of thought crush, whether by asking us to apprehend up to three diegetic levels simultaneously, as in "Acorn Antiques," or by evoking a metafictional tussle between an "official" and "saboteur" narration, as in the "Stayin' Alive" sketch from *Airplane!* (both chapter 2).

## Ethos

Considering the *ethos* of an instance of comedy is to consider its invitation to a community of laughter. Part of this is to think of comedy as appealing to particular values that we are expected, perhaps even demanded, to share. Our "Toilet Party" sequence from *The Phantom of Liberty*, for example, addresses a viewer who finds the niceties of dinner parties tiresome and the veil cast over lower bodily function absurd. "Awkward Conversation" asks its audience to share its disdain for adolescent irony as a tool of social enforcement. The appeal to values is perhaps most striking in cases of satire, such as these, where comic pleasure is conditional on accepting the premise that a satirical target is fair game.

Beyond satire, however, to see comedy as involving an invitation to community is to recognize that humor is not just an intellectual construction and/or a means of emotional manipulation but a form of human-to-human address. Ted Cohen, mentioned previously, brings out this dimension when he emphasizes the intimacy longed for, and realized, through jokes, which call upon a shared understanding, a shared way of seeing, or at least an invitation, in some way, to join hands (Cohen: 1999). This is the key reason, beyond technical capacity, why robots seem destined forever to be incapable of humor, in the fullest sense of the word. However ingenious a verbal formulation might be concocted by artificial intelligence, it is difficult to see how a computer could manifest this sort of intimacy, unless perhaps we imagine these efforts to be reflecting, indirectly, the distributed wit of a human programmer. You can't exactly bond with a machine.

One almost universal convention of sketch comedy is testament to the importance of this dimension, namely, that we are typically expected to recognize and perhaps even in some way identify with the main performers. The two are connected: identification *of* the troupe allows for identification *with* the troupe, with its collective way of seeing, its way of being, and its sense of humor (whether madcap, deadpan, irreverent, dark, or gregarious). Budgetary implications aside, it's possible to imagine a sketch show where each of the skits involves new and previously unknown actors. However, the effect would be quite unlike the usual situation, where between two and six identifiable members of a comic troupe play all the main characters, putting on different costumes, accents, perhaps even an array of silly walks, to perform their various roles. One challenge for makers of sketch comedy is that with each skit you need to begin again. However, having recognized performers means not having to build quite from scratch. It allows, for one thing, a shorthand, as we saw in the casting of affable "nice guy" Michael Palin as the customer in "Argument Clinic" (chapter 3). We found that sketch to culminate in the most overt acknowledgment of Monty Python as a troupe, when the gang reassembles to perform something like a stage bow, clasping one another by the shoulder under the premise of making arrests for crimes against comedy.

The recurrence of performers between sketches, calling upon our recognition of their different comic personae and temperaments, does not just give a sketch show, otherwise a patchwork of comic scenes, a tentative unity, although it *is* important that we feel we are not simply dipping in and out of alien bits and pieces, as we might in the hypothetical case of a sketch show without a troupe. Sketch performers are considerably different than jobbing actors who happen to be acting a comedic role. With a troupe, we are asked to understand that the performers have a history and bond with one another and that they are in some sense members of a creative community who offer their material for our appreciation. We are also often asked to imagine that they are *having fun* in this creative endeavor. This may be a fantasy, but it is a powerful one and important, in many cases, for comedians to convey since it issues a virtual call for us to join them, to have fun *with* them, to enjoy the fun they are (ostensibly) having. It can be alienating, of course, even irritating, to see others having fun and to find oneself excluded—and, a different problem, it is maddening to intuit that the fun is being faked. These are issues that screen comedy needs perpetually to overcome.

There is, however, an acknowledgment in sketch comedy, more or less continuous, that roles are being *performed*. The main players in a comic troupe do not, on the whole, shrink into their characters but wear them ostentatiously. The script for the "Dead Parrot" sketch (discussed in the introduction) may start by saying that a man walks into a pet shop, but that is misleading. *John Cleese* walks into a pet shop, with a John Cleese look on his face, and that's a quite different matter. Jordan Peele and Keegan-Michael Key immediately stand out from the supporting cast around the table in "Awkward Conversation" (discussed in chapter 1) because they are wearing wigs just the wrong side of naturalistic. Unflattering as they are, the wigs are not exactly played for laughs; they acknowledge the playing of roles. We see that they know that *we* know they are putting it on. What's more, Key and Peele give the distinct impression, especially as the sketch moves into the passage of reverse-field cutting, of playing to one another. The two leads almost seem to be trying to outdo each other with their gurning, turning the amplification dial up higher, as if trying to make one another laugh. There seems to be, for instance, a twinkle of suppressed mirth in Jordan Peele's face when his fellow performer forcefully seizes his head, gripping and twisting it with all the sadistic license the occasion provides. It's a marvel that he doesn't crack up.

Indeed, although "character" in sketch comedy is never the intact vessel to which straight drama aspires, there are infrequent occasions when a performer "breaks character" by laughing—what the British call "corpsing." We noted instances of this with Eddie Murphy in *Saturday Night Live* and Victoria Wood in "Acorn Antiques." It is an unspoken law of comedy that one can never give the impression of "corpsing" on purpose—which only goes to show its advantage, that it gives the audience a glimpse of the authentic performer behind the mask. Just as Aristotle's *ethos* of oratory alludes to the "personal character" of the speaker, so the *ethos* of comedy is to offer the comedian as human, companionate, convivial.

## Pathos

It is not sufficient, however, to consider only the realm of suggestions and ideas, and the invitation to community, when trying to articulate how something is funny. Just as Aristotle observed the importance, in oratory, of putting the audience in a certain frame of mind that is sympathetic to the argument being made, so comedy needs to put its audience in a comic frame of mind. The *pathos*, or affective dimension, of comic rhetoric is the means by which it moves us towards laughter.

Music often plays a decisive role in the way sketches put us "in the mood." We saw this most exuberantly in the Morecambe and Wise sketch, where the upbeat, brassy tones of "The Stripper" helped turn a mundane morning ritual into a fiesta (chapter 4). Elsewhere, we found a unique mood fostered by the choice of Harry Nilsson's "Without You" for the *Smack the Pony* singalong (chapter 5). Its earnest strains do not exactly function as counterpoint since we take them to reflect something of the despondency that the main character is trying, in her way, to convey, perhaps to shake. There is a tone of what we might call comic poignancy that comes not from the song itself but from the contrast between its full-throated expression of emotion against this character's relative timidity, the self-defeating social reserve we witness in her self-conscious glances and aborted runs.

Beyond the direct use of music, we have noted throughout this book the musical aspects of comedy. It has become a truism to say that comedy is "all about timing." Of course, it is not *all* about timing, but the contribution of features such as pace, rhythm, and phrasing can hardly be overstated. We observed, for instance, in the "Four Yorkshiremen" sketch (chapter 5), that the sense of compulsive, repetitive one-upmanship is carried through echoing of syntactical forms (e.g., "'Ouse? You were lucky"; "Room? You were lucky") but that the rhythm of dialogue is carefully modulated to avoid monotony and to keep the development surprising.

Elsewhere, we found the comic energy of "Sir Digby Chicken-Caesar" (chapter 1), as our protagonist flees the scene of a crime, to derive from qualities of acceleration and simultaneity and to disorienting shifts in viewpoint that fostered a tone of giddiness—for instance, the way the rattling tempo with which his inner monologue is delivered ("On a lonely planet spinning its way to damnation amid the fear and despair of a broken human race . . .") is combined with the injection of energy provided by a whirling body-mount camera. Like a funfair ride, the effect is visceral, not merely intellectual.

Susanne K. Langer is a rare theorist who has gestured towards this aspect of comedy. Langer finds comedy uniquely poised to embody and elicit a "a surge of vital feeling" (1977: 340). What distinguishes comedy from other artistic forms, for her, is its embodiment of a "rhythm" of what she calls "sheer vitality" (332). Langer finds comedy speaking to a deep biological instinct, common to all organic matter, for self-preservation and self-restoration. If that suggestion sounds a touch New Age and far-fetched (and it could be reductive in its own way if that was *all* comedy was taken to be), we can readily discern something like this in the way "Sir Digby," for instance, is structured episodically as a series of scrapes, each one culminating in a resplendent burst of *The Devil's Gallop* as Sir Digby flees the scene, a perversely exuberant flight from responsibility. This is Langer's "comic rhythm," with its alternation between "upset and recovery" (331). We found a related expression of buoyancy, of bouncing back, in the succession of "boomerang gags" that pervaded the disco sequence in *Airplane!* (chapter 2). What we found important here was the *feeling* of the irrepressible.

Recalling Langer's notion of a "surge," we had occasion, as well, in this book to observe the frequency with which comedy manifests precipitous accumulation, a feeling of acceleration. The comic surge may take the form of a kind of sensory pile-on, as in the frenetic montage and eventual cosmic explosion with which "Price War" culminates (chapter 5), or a sudden lurch, such as the darting dance movement of Captain Billing-Smythe and Daisy as they plough through the remaining house ornaments in "Spiffington Manse" (chapter 2). The sensation, in this case, is not relief but exhilaration. Richard Dyer's explanation of the appeal of musicals, and of entertainment more widely, is that they offer a sense of "what utopia would feel like" (2002: 20, my italics). For Dyer, the dominant feelings elicited by entertainment, which he categorizes as energy, abundance, intensity, transparency, and community, respond and offer a counterweight to real-world problems of exhaustion, scarcity, dreariness, manipulation, and fragmentation. Applied to comedy as a mode of entertainment, Dyer's functional hypothesis could end up being a socially oriented version of the relief theory of humor. Nonetheless, it is worth considering, as part of what I am calling humor's *pathos*, how comedy works to engineer "utopian feeling." We found something like this offered by the monks sketch from *Big Train* (discussed in the introduction), with Brother Mark's absurdly forgiving reaction to the hoax, and in the "Breakfast" sketch, again (chapter 4), with its utopian synthesis of the domestic, the theatrical, and the erotic, as an antidote to the tolls of bourgeois marriage.

Accounting for the *pathos* of humor, especially, requires close and vivid evocation of how a comic instance unfolds, moment by moment. It is this dimension, accordingly, that has proved elusive for critics and theorists who crave a shortcut into grasping what makes us laugh. There is no essence of humor, and it can certainly not be found in the logic, structure, or values extracted from a set of comic specimens. The humor of comedy emerges from the way performers move; how they deliver their lines; how they are lit, framed, and edited; how they are clothed; and how the set is dressed—and so on, and so forth. These aspects don't all compel laughter, but they help inspire it, generating an atmosphere conducive to mirth.

## Comedy in Three Dimensions

The three "dimensions" summarized above are interlinked aspects of comic rhetoric. My hope is that highlighting that all three aspects are operative in humor should at least deter the kind of reductive account that has tended to pass for comic analysis. Any account has to end somewhere, has to be nonexhaustive, but perhaps, used as a rough checklist, these "three dimensions" might at least urge analysts not to draw a line too hastily and not to fixate on a single dimension (say, the logic or structure of comedy, without considering how it unfolds and how it addresses its audience). There is no reason, on the other hand, to assume that each of these aspects will carry equal weight in any given instance. There might be more to say about one and less about the others. Equally, it offers no way to predict the channels by which the *ethos*, *logos*, and *pathos* of a comic instance will be realized. The onus remains on the analyst to trust her or his experience, to reflect honestly upon it, to observe closely and carefully, and to strive to find the apposite words to convey the humor of the work.

What I want to suggest here, and what I ultimately hope to have shown in this book, is, first, that humor is not the disposable phenomenon that it is often assumed to be and, second, that it is capable of being analyzed in a spirit that does justice to it. At some points in this book, including this concluding chapter, I have had occasion to return to instances that I have discussed before, finding more to say. The very possibility of this suggests that accomplished works of humor, like other works of art, contain many facets, that they are capable of withstanding, indeed may reward, multiple returns and sustained consideration. This is another reason for thinking of comic rhetoric as having dimensions: the point being that humor is substantial, not thin, not throwaway, even if it sometimes is constructed to seem offhand and casual. Articulating the satisfactions that comedy affords, and identifying how these have been attained, is for this reason quite a challenge. Trying to say how something is funny might still strike some as a peculiar thing to want to do. But it seems to me an imperative if we want to understand the artistry of comedy and the specificity of humor as a phenomenon, its place in our culture and in our lives.

# Works Cited

Aristotle, 2004 [322 B.C.]. *Rhetoric*. Trans. W. D. Ross. Dover.
Bergson, H., 2005 [1901]. *Laughter: An Essay on the Meaning of the Comic*. Trans. Cloudsley Brereton and Fred Rothwell. Dover.
Brighouse, H., 2006. "Why Is an Argument Clinic Less Silly Than an Abuse Clinic or a Contradiction Clinic?" in Hardcastle, G. & Reisch, G. (eds.), *Monty Python and Philosophy: Nudge Nudge, Think Think!* Open Court, 53–63.
Cavell, S., 2005. "The Good of Film" in Rothman, W. (ed.), *Cavell on Film*, State University of New York Press.
Chapman, G., Cleese, J., Gilliam, T., Idle, E., Jones, T., Palin, M., with McCabe, B., 2003. *The Pythons Autobiography by the Pythons*. Orion.
Clayton, A., 2007. *The Body in Hollywood Slapstick*. McFarland.
Clayton, A., 2013. "Why Comedy Is at Home on Television" in Jacobs, J., and Peacock, S. (eds.), *Television Aesthetics and Style*, Bloomsbury, 79–92.
Clayton, A., 2015. "V. F. Perkins: Aesthetic Suspense" in Pomerance, M., and Palmer, R. B. (eds.), *Thinking in the Dark: Cinema, Theory, Practice*, Rutgers University Press, 208–16.
Cohen, T., 1999. *Jokes: Philosophical Thoughts on Joking Matters*. University of Chicago Press.
Dewey, J., 2008 [1889]. *The Early Works, 1882–1898*, vol. 3. Southern Illinois University Press.
Durgnat, R., 1964. "The Mass-Media—A Highbrow Illiteracy?" *Views* 4, Spring, 49–59.
Dyer, R., 2002. *Only Entertainment*. Psychology.
Freud, S., 1922. *Jokes and Their Relation to the Unconscious*. Routledge and Kegan Paul.
Fried, M., 1988. *Absorption and Theatricality: Painting and Beholder in the Age of Diderot*. University of Chicago Press.
Gervais, M., & Wilson, D. S., 2005. "The Evolution and Functions of Laughter and Humor: A Synthetic Approach." *Quarterly Review of Biology* 80, 395–430.
Hobbes, T., 2010 [1650]. *The Treatise on Human Nature and That on Liberty and Necessity*. Nabu.

Humphries, R., 1995. "Lacan and the Ostrich: Desire and Narration in Buñuel's *Le Fantôme de la Liberté.*" *American Imago* 52, no. 2, Summer, 191–203.

Hutcheon, L., 2000. *A Theory of Parody: The Teachings of Twentieth-Century Art Forms.* University of Illinois Press.

Kant, I., 2007 [1790]. *Critique of Judgment.* Cosimo.

Koestler, A., 1964. *The Act of Creation.* Macmillan.

Langer, S., 1977. *Feeling and Form: A Theory of Art Developed from Philosophy in a New Key.* Macmillan.

McGraw, P., & Warren, C., 2010. "Benign Violations: Making Immoral Behaviour Funny." *Psychological Science* 21, 1141–49.

Morreall, J., 1983. *Taking Laughter Seriously.* State University of New York Press.

Morreall, J. (ed.). 1986. *The Philosophy of Laughter and Humor.* State University of New York Press.

Schopenhauer, A., 2000 [1883]. *The World as Will and Representation, Vol. 1.* Trans. E. F. J. Payne. Dover.

Suleiman, S., 1978. "Freedom and Necessity: Narrative Structure in *The Phantom of Liberty.*" *Quarterly Review of Film Studies* 3.3, Summer, 277–95.

Tobias, J., 1998. "Buñuel's Net Work: Performative Doubles in the Impossible Narrative of *The Phantom of Liberty.*" *Film Quarterly* 52, no. 2, Winter, 10–22.

Veatch, T. C., 1998. "A Theory of Humor." *HUMOR: International Journal of Humor Research* 11, no. 2.

White, E. B., & White, K. B., 1941. Preface to *A Subtreasury of American Humor.* Coward-McCann.

Wittgenstein, L., 1953. *Philosophical Investigations.* Trans. E. Anscombe. Blackwell.

Wittgenstein, L. (ed. Cyril Barrett), 1966. *Lectures & Conversations on Aesthetics, Psychology and Religious Belief.* Blackwell.

Wittgenstein, L., 1979. *Remarks on Frazer's Golden Bough.* Trans. A. C. Miles. Brynmill.

Wittgenstein, L., 1993. *Philosophical Occasions, 1912–1951.* Trans. James C. Klagge and Alfred Nordmann. Hackett.

Wittusen, C., 2010. "Philosophical Method as a Technique of Art." *Literature and Aesthetics* 20, no. 2.

Wood, M., 2000. "Down with Liberty." *Sight and Sound,* September, 30–33.

# Index

acceleration, 25, 34, 43, 117–118, 133
Acorn Antiques (*Victoria Wood* sketch), 57–65, 129, 132
*Airplane!*, 2–57, 130, 133
Aristotle, 23, 128, 132
*At Last the 1948 Show*, 107–113
Atkinson, Rowan, 79–82
Awkward Conversation (*Key and Peele* sketch), 33–40, 89, 120, 130, 131

Bergson, Henri, 16–18, 33–40, 46–47
Boardroom (*Errand Boy* sketch), 95–101
Breakfast (*Morecambe and Wise* sketch), 89–95, 132, 134
Brighouse, Harry, 71, 73–74
Brooke-Taylor, Tim, 107, 108, 112
Brown, James, 102–106, 129

Cavell, Stanley, 118–119
Chapman, Graham, 2, 71, 73, 75, 77, 107, 108
choreography, 27, 51, 64, 69–70, 91–95
Clayton, Alex, 32, 92, 96–97, 109
Cleese, John, 1–7, 71–72, 75, 76, 77, 107, 108, 109, 110, 131
clumsiness, 59, 62, 66–70
Cohen, Ted, 127, 130
comic rhythm, 4, 6, 43, 68, 96, 98, 104, 112, 115, 128, 132–133

comic structure, 32, 34–35, 73, 77, 89, 101, 109–112, 122, 133, 134
comic theory, 4, 9–48, 54, 127, 134
disorientation, 44–45, 116, 117, 113, 133

Dead Parrot (*Monty Python* sketch), 1–7, 129, 131
density, 1, 5–6, 45, 49, 59, 64, 69, 97, 129
Dewey, John, 11–12, 14, 21
Durgnat, Raymond, 101–102
Dyer, Richard, 133–134

*Errand Boy, The*, 95–101, 129
escalation, 35, 67–70, 107, 109, 110–111, 117, 120
*ethos* [of humor], 128, 130–132, 134
excess, 35, 40, 65–66, 70, 86, 113, 117–118, 129
exhilaration, 45, 62, 95, 133

Feldman, Marty, 107, 108, 109, 112
Four Yorkshiremen (*At Last the 1948 Show* sketch), 107–113, 133
Freud, Sigmund, 12
Fried, Michael, 91

Gerald the Gorilla (*Not the Nine O'Clock News* sketch), 77–83, 86, 87, 129

gesture, 7, 26, 36, 38, 39, 43, 44, 46, 60, 64, 66, 69, 70, 80, 81, 86, 96, 97, 98, 99, 110, 124
Gilliam, Terry, 76
Grotesque, 3, 83, 110, 117

Hobbes, Thomas, 9–11, 15, 21, 22–27
Hot Tub (*Saturday Night Live* sketch), 101–106, 132
Hutcheon, Linda, 54

Idle, Eric, 73, 76, 77
  comic imagery, 3, 34, 35, 38, 94, 97, 105, 109–110, 113
  mimicry, 29, 33, 57–58, 103–106, 113
Imrie, Celia, 57, 58, 59, 60, 64
incongruity theory of humor, 9, 12–13, 15, 21–22, 40–44, 46, 51–52, 129

Jones, Terry, 76

Kant, Immanuel, 28, 30–33
*Key and Peele*, 34–40, 89, 120, 131, 132
Key, Michael-Keegan, 34, 35, 37, 131
Koestler, Arthur, 12, 53

Langer, Susanne, 133
Lewis, Jerry, 95–101, 129
*Little Britain*, 22–28, 129
*logos* [of humor], 128–130, 134
Lucas, Matt, 22, 23, 28

Mackichan, Doon, 118, 119, 121, 122, 123, 124, 125
McGraw, Peter & Warren, Caleb, 20
*Micallef Program, The*, 65–70
Micallef, Shaun, 66, 68, 69
Mitchell, David, 41, 42, 89
Monks' Humor (*Big Train* sketch), 28–33, 134
*Monty Python's Flying Circus*, 1–7, 71–77, 87, 89, 107, 129, 131
*Morecambe and Wise Show, The*, 89–95, 132, 134

Morecambe, Eric, 89, 90, 91, 92, 93, 94, 95
Morreall, John, 9, 12, 23, 128
Murphy, Eddie, 102, 103, 104, 105, 106, 107

pace, 43, 45, 113, 115, 117, 133
Palin, Michael, 1, 2, 71, 72, 73, 74, 75, 76, 131
parody, 31–32, 38, 49–50, 54, 57–58, 66–67, 89, 105, 113, 129–130
*pathos* [of humor], 128, 132–134
Peele, Jordan, 34, 35, 37, 131
*Phantom of Liberty, The*, 83–87, 129, 130
Phillips, Sally, 118, 119, 121, 122, 123, 124, 125
pretense, 28, 105, 124, 125
Price War (*Tim and Eric* sketch), 113–118, 129, 133

*Raiders of the Lost Ark*, 10–13
relief theory of humor, 9, 11–12, 13, 16, 30–33, 133, 134
repetition, 35, 36, 37, 39, 65–66, 68, 92, 98, 104, 109

satire, 35, 39–40, 50, 58, 114, 130
*Saturday Night Live* 101–106, 132
Schopenhauer, Arthur, 15, 21, 40–44, 46
Singing Contest (*Smack the Pony* sketch), 118–125, 132
skepticism, 75–76, 77, 87, 118–119
*Smack the Pony*, 118–125, 132
Smith, Mel, 78, 79, 82
Spiffington Manse (*Micallef* sketch), 65–70, 129, 133
Stayin' Alive (*Airplane* sketch), 49–57, 130, 133
superiority theory of humor, 9–11, 13, 15, 22–28
Swimming Pool (*Little Britain* sketch), 22–28

*That Mitchell and Webb Look*, 40–45, 89, 133
thought experiment, 19, 71, 75, 77–80, 83–84, 85–87
*Tim and Eric Awesome Show, Great Job!*, 113–118, 129, 133
Toilet Party (*Phantom of Liberty* sketch), 83–87, 129, 130

variety theatre, 77, 89–90
Veatch, Thomas, 20–21

*Victoria Wood: As Seen on TV*, 57–65, 129, 132

Walliams, David, 22, 23, 27–28
Walters, Julie, 58, 59, 60, 63, 64
Webb, Robert, 41, 44, 45, 89
Wise, Ernie, 89, 90, 91, 92, 93, 94, 95, 132
Wittgenstein, Ludwig, 1, 18–20, 46, 77–79
Wood, Victoria, 57, 59, 132

Also in the series

William Rothman, editor, *Cavell on Film*

J. David Slocum, editor, *Rebel Without a Cause*

Joe McElhaney, *The Death of Classical Cinema*

Kirsten Moana Thompson, *Apocalyptic Dread*

Frances Gateward, editor, *Seoul Searching*

Michael Atkinson, editor, *Exile Cinema*

Paul S. Moore, *Now Playing*

Robin L. Murray and Joseph K. Heumann, *Ecology and Popular Film*

William Rothman, editor, *Three Documentary Filmmakers*

Sean Griffin, editor, *Hetero*

Jean-Michel Frodon, editor, *Cinema and the Shoah*

Carolyn Jess-Cooke and Constantine Verevis, editors, *Second Takes*

Matthew Solomon, editor, *Fantastic Voyages of the Cinematic Imagination*

R. Barton Palmer and David Boyd, editors, *Hitchcock at the Source*

William Rothman, *Hitchcock: The Murderous Gaze, Second Edition*

Joanna Hearne, *Native Recognition*

Marc Raymond, *Hollywood's New Yorker*

Steven Rybin and Will Scheibel, editors, *Lonely Places, Dangerous Ground*

Claire Perkins and Constantine Verevis, editors, *B Is for Bad Cinema*

Dominic Lennard, *Bad Seeds and Holy Terrors*

Rosie Thomas, *Bombay before Bollywood*

Scott M. MacDonald, *Binghamton Babylon*

Sudhir Mahadevan, *A Very Old Machine*

David Greven, *Ghost Faces*

James S. Williams, *Encounters with Godard*

William H. Epstein and R. Barton Palmer, editors, *Invented Lives, Imagined Communities*

Lee Carruthers, *Doing Time*

Rebecca Meyers, William Rothman, and Charles Warren, editors, *Looking with Robert Gardner*

Belinda Smaill, *Regarding Life*

Douglas McFarland and Wesley King, editors, *John Huston as Adaptor*
R. Barton Palmer, Homer B. Pettey, and Steven M. Sanders, editors, *Hitchcock's Moral Gaze*
Nenad Jovanovic, *Brechtian Cinemas*
Will Scheibel, *American Stranger*
Amy Rust, *Passionate Detachments*
Steven Rybin, *Gestures of Love*
Seth Friedman, *Are You Watching Closely?*
Roger Rawlings, *Ripping England!*
Michael DeAngelis, *Rx Hollywood*
Ricardo E. Zulueta, *Queer Art Camp Superstar*
John Caruana and Mark Cauchi, editors, *Immanent Frames*
Nathan Holmes, *Welcome to Fear City*
Homer B. Pettey and R. Barton Palmer, editors, *Rule, Britannia!*
Milo Sweedler, *Rumble and Crash*
Ken Windrum, *From El Dorado to Lost Horizons*
Matthew Lau, *Sounds Like Helicopters*
Dominic Lennard, *Brute Force*
William Rothman, *Tuitions and Intuitions*
Michael Hammond, *The Great War in Hollywood Memory, 1918–1939*
Burke Hilsabeck, *The Slapstick Camera*
Niels Niessen, *Miraculous Realism*

www.ingramcontent.com/pod-product-compliance
Lightning Source LLC
Chambersburg PA
CBHW021144230426
43667CB00005B/249